OPEN SKY

T0209666

RADICAL THINKERS }

SET 1 ($12/£6/$14CAN)

MINIMA MORALIA
Reflections on a Damaged Life
THEODOR ADORNO
ISBN-13: 978 1 84467 051 2

FOR MARX
LOUIS ALTHUSSER
ISBN-13: 978 1 84467 052 9

THE SYSTEM OF OBJECTS
JEAN BAUDRILLARD
ISBN-13: 978 1 84467 053 6

LIBERALISM AND DEMOCRACY
NORBERTO BOBBIO
ISBN-13: 978 1 84467 062 8

THE POLITICS OF FRIENDSHIP
JACQUES DERRIDA
ISBN-13: 978 1 84467 054 3

THE FUNCTION OF CRITICISM
TERRY EAGLETON
ISBN-13: 978 1 84467 055 0

SIGNS TAKEN FOR WONDERS
On the Sociology of Literary Forms
FRANCO MORETTI
ISBN-13: 978 1 84467 056 7

THE RETURN OF THE POLITICAL
CHANTAL MOUFFE
ISBN-13: 978 1 84467 057 4

SEXUALITY IN THE FIELD OF VISION
JACQUELINE ROSE
ISBN-13: 978 1 84467 058 1

THE INFORMATION BOMB
PAUL VIRILIO
ISBN-13: 978 1 84467 059 8

CULTURE AND MATERIALISM
RAYMOND WILLIAMS
ISBN-13: 978 1 84467 060 4

THE METASTASES OF ENJOYMENT
On Women and Causality
SLAVOJ ŽIŽEK
ISBN-13: 978 1 84467 061 1

SET 2 ($12.95/£6.99/$17CAN)

AESTHETICS AND POLITICS
THEODOR ADORNO, WALTER BENJAMIN, ERNST BLOCH, BERTOLT BRECHT, GEORG LUKÁCS
ISBN-13: 978 1 84467 570 8

INFANCY AND HISTORY
On the Destruction of Experience
GIORGIO AGAMBEN
ISBN-13: 978 1 84467 571 5

POLITICS AND HISTORY
Montesquieu, Rousseau, Marx
LOUIS ALTHUSSER
ISBN-13: 978 1 84467 572 2

FRAGMENTS
JEAN BAUDRILLARD
ISBN-13: 978 1 84467 573 9

LOGICS OF DISINTEGRATION
Poststructuralist Thought and the Claims of Critical Theory
PETER DEWS
ISBN-13: 978 1 84467 574 6

LATE MARXISM
Adorno, Or, The Persistence of the Dialectic
FREDRIC JAMESON
ISBN-13: 978 1 84467 575 3

EMANCIPATION(S)
ERNESTO LACLAU
ISBN-13: 978 1 84467 576 0

THE POLITICAL DESCARTES
Reason, Ideology and the Bourgeois Project
ANTONIO NEGRI
ISBN-13: 978 1 84467 582 1

ON THE SHORES OF POLITICS
JACQUES RANCIÈRE
ISBN-13: 978 1 84467 577 7

STRATEGY OF DECEPTION
PAUL VIRILIO
ISBN-13: 978 1 84467 578 4

POLITICS OF MODERNISM
Against the New Conformists
RAYMOND WILLIAMS
ISBN-13: 978 1 84467 580 7

THE INDIVISIBLE REMAINDER
On Schelling and Related Matters
SLAVOJ ŽIŽEK
ISBN-13: 978 1 84467 581 4

OPEN SKY

Paul Virilio

Translated by Julie Rose

VERSO

London • New York

This translation was completed with the assistance of the Australia Council

First published by Verso 1997
This edition published by Verso 2008
Copyright © Verso 2008
Translation © Julie Rose 1997
First published as *La vitesse de libération*
Copyright © Editions Galilée 1995

1 3 5 7 9 10 8 6 4 2

Verso
UK: 6 Meard Street, London W1F 0EG
USA: 180 Varick Street, New York, NY 10014-4606
www.versobooks.com

Verso is the imprint of New Left Books

ISBN-13: 978-1-84467-208-0

British Library Cataloguing in Publication Data
A catalogue record for this book is available from the British Library

Library of Congress Cataloging-in-Publication Data
A catalog record for this book is available from the Library of Congress

Printed and bound by ScandBook AB, Sweden

Contents

One day
the day will come
when the day won't come

INTRODUCTION

The blue sky above us is the optical layer of the atmosphere, the great lens of the terrestrial globe, its brilliant retina.

From ultra-marine, beyond the sea, to ultra-sky, the horizon divides opacity from transparency. It is just one small step from earth-matter to space-light – a leap or a take-off able to free us for a moment from gravity.

But the horizon, the *skyline*, is not only a launch pad. It is also the very first littoral, a vertical littoral, the one which absolutely separates 'the void' from 'the full'. Unremarked invention of the art of painting and of distinguishing a 'form' from a 'background', the *ground line* anticipates from afar the maritime shore – the 'Azure Coast', that horizontal seaboard that so often causes us to lose sight of the zenithal perspective.

Besides, the entire history of Quattrocento perspectives is only ever a story of struggle, of the battle of geometers vying to make us forget the 'high' and the 'low' by pushing the 'near' and the 'far', a *vanishing-point* that literally fascinated them, even though our vision is actually determined by our weight and oriented by the pull of earth's gravity, by the classic distinction between *zenith* and *nadir*.

The original reference point for sight is therefore not what the Italian masters said it was, that of vanishing lines converging on the horizon, but one bound up with the delicate balancing act of a universal attraction which imposes on us its gearing towards the centre of the Earth, at the risk of our falling.

As Victor Hugo put it: *The rope doesn't hang, the Earth pulls.*

In this age of the sudden pollution of the atmosphere, it is about time we revised our perception of appearances. *To raise your eyes to the heavens* could become more than a sign of helplessness or exasperation.

A secret perspective is, in fact, hidden *on high.*

A different kind of vanishing act from that performed by the ozone is hidden behind the clouds. The breakaway of the Wright brothers on their first take-off from the beach at Kitty Hawk or, perhaps, the liftoff of the Apollo 11 mission at Cape Canaveral, show us another way, an exotic reorganization of sight that would finally take account of a possible *fall upwards* brought on by the recent acquisition of the speed of liberation from gravity: orbital speed at 28,000 kilometres per hour.

Preoccupied as we are, at the end of the millennium, with developing the absolute speed of our modern *real-time* transmission tools, we too often forget the comparable historic importance of this other limit-speed, the one which has enabled us to escape the *real space* of our planet and so to 'fall upwards'.

Reverse vertigo that may well force us to change the way we think about the landscape and about the human environment.

So not only has our generation just discovered a hole in the thin layer of ozone that once protected us from cosmic rays; it has also just poked another one in the blue, for, from now on, *our sky is vanishing.*

The vanishing-point at the horizon of the Quattrocento is now coupled with that of the Novecento: *today, there is a way out up above.* An artificial counter-gravity allowing man to shed telluric gravity, the stability of gravitational space that has always oriented man's habitual activities.

Everything is being turned on its head at this *fin de siècle* – not only geopolitical boundaries but those of perspective geometry.

Arse over heels! Appearances generally and those of art in particular are being deconstructed – but so is the sudden transparency of the world's landscape.

Soon we will have to learn to fly, to swim in the ether.

If we really want to reorient our daily lives, we will soon need to change our bearings, to shift our sights 'upwards'.

If the loss of the inaccessible far reaches is accompanied by a media proximity that owes everything to the speed of light, we shall also pretty soon have to get used to the distortion of appearances caused by the *real-time perspective* of telecommunications, a perspective in which the old line of the horizon curls itself inside the frame of the screen, optoelectronics supplanting the optics of our telescopes!

And this is all in preparation for astrophysics' great surprise: *beyond earth's pull, there is no space worthy of the name, but only time!* A kind of time that will take on cosmic reality single-handed.

Indeed, have not certain astronomers and mathematicians recently asserted that time has its own inertia, that time is in fact matter, a different kind of material?[1]

Once astrophysicists stop talking exclusively about 'space-time' and start talking about 'space-time-matter', they help to lock extension and duration into the web of a different kind of cosmic materiality, unrelated to our experience of the trinity of matter, space and time.[2]

By the same token introducing a third kind of interval of the 'light' type alongside those of 'space' and 'time', they engineer the emergence of a new conception of time, which is no longer exclusively the time of classic chronological *succession*, but now a time of (chronoscopic) *exposure* of the duration of events at the speed of light – something certain writers interested in police investigation methods long ago divined. Indeed if, according to Emile Gaboriau's sleuth, *'time is just one more obscurity'* that gradually wipes out all the clues and winds up concealing the truth of the facts, then *speed is time's light*, its sole 'light' and one can no longer consider duration – any duration or any physical extension – without the help of the illumination of an absolute speed that changes our understanding of time.

To the *passing* time of the longest durations, we now add accordingly a time that is *exposed* instantaneously: the time of the shortest durations in the realms of electromagnetism and of gravity.

It is easy to imagine the havoc wreaked by this new 'conception of the world', its effects on the very nature of **perspective** and so on the orientation of human activities: *if time is matter, what is space?*

These days it is not the 'geographic' space of the golden hills of Tuscany under the Italian Renaissance sun, a 'geometric' space that once shaped a durable vision of the near world through the window of perspective. It is now the space over the seas and beyond the sky, this so-called 'cosmic space' whose obscurity is no longer so much a matter of lack of sun as of *the night of a spaceless time* without measurable extent apart from seasonless 'light-years', since alternation of night and day is now saddled with *an alternation of terrestrial space and its extraterrestrial absence.*

So the temporal day of our *matter-years* will be joined by a night of spaceless *light-years*, the obscure reign of an absent mass that will finally be identified with universal time, that is to say, with an otherworldly temporality bearing no relation to the fundamentally 'spatio-temporal' nature of our activities within the space of a planet *suspended in time*; the ether of 'time-light' being in no way analogous to our usual calculation of duration and geophysical span.

Listen to the physicists specializing in this famous absent mass: 'What are these particles that form the dark mass, the substantial non-luminous part of the Universe? It is tempting to assume that the dark rings of the galaxies are made of supernatant baryons. These baryons would be found in the compact form of small dark stars – brown dwarfs – but such celestial objects can only make up a small part of the dark matter of the Universe.'[3]

The 'rest' of this cosmic darkness, so vast that it defies the scientific imagination, would then be *the absent mass of time*, would it not? This cosmic time that escapes our astronomic observation, in also escaping the absolute but finite speed of light? Universal temporality that remains in 'the shadow' of an acceleration limited to 300,000 kilometres a second.

In such hypothetical conditions, contemporary research into the famous **big bang** might be said to be an illusion, an optical illusion of cosmology!

How can we hope to contemplate *live* – thanks to *Indra*, the new machine of the great national **heavy ion** accelerator – *the creation of space-time-matter* fifteen billion years ago, if the inertia of universal time screens out all observation due to the very finite nature of the speed of light, of this **time–light** that illuminates events, while being at the same time quite incapable of illuminating itself?

Besides, in baptizing a technological device designed to pick up the very first signals of the universe *Indra*, from the name of the Vedic god of the heavens, our scientific elders overlooked the discontinuity that apparently exists between space-time subject to earth's gravity and the space-time of the extraterrestrial otherworld.

After 'anthropocentrism' and 'geocentrism', our contemporary *savants* seem now to be in the grip of a new kind of illuminism, or rather **luminocentrism**, capable of hoodwinking them about the profound nature of space and of time, the old perspective of the real space of the Quattrocento once again blocking the perspective of the real time of a horizonless cosmos.

But to conclude this eminently probabilist introduction, we might return to our new 'côte d'Azur', to this zenithal shore that so clearly partitions off the sphere of a *space-matter* subject to earth's gravity from the extraterrestrial *time-light* whose depth dissimulates the very density of time, the dark mass of universal time ultimately giving the optical layer of our planet its azure colour.

If *nature* abhors a vacuum, so too does *la grandeur-nature* (life-size). Without weight or measure, there is no 'nature' any more or, at least, no *idea* of nature. Without a distant horizon, there is no longer any possibility of glimpsing reality; we drop into the time of a fall akin to that of the fallen angels and the earth's horizon then becomes just another 'Baie des Anges'. Philosophical let-down in which the *idea of nature* of the Age of Enlightenment is eradicated, along with the *idea of the real* in the age of the speed of light.

PART 1

THE THIRD INTERVAL

'Without even leaving, we are already no longer there.'

Nikolai Gogol

Critical *mass*, critical *moment*, critical *temperature*. You don't hear much about critical *space*, though. Why is this if not because we have not yet digested relativity, the very notion of space-time?

And yet critical space, and critical expanse, are now everywhere, due to the acceleration of communications tools that *obliterate the Atlantic* (Concorde), *reduce France to a square one and a half hours across* (Airbus) or *gain time over time* with the TGV, the various advertising slogans signalling perfectly the shrinking of geophysical space of which we are the beneficiaries but also, sometimes, the unwitting victims.

As for telecommunications tools, not content to limit extension, they are also eradicating all duration, any extension of time in the transmission of messages, images.

Mass transportation revolution of the nineteenth century, broadcasting revolution of the twentieth – a mutation and a commutation that affect both public and domestic space at the same time, to the point where we are left in some uncertainty as to their very reality, since the urbanization of *real space* is currently giving way to a preliminary urbanization of *real time*, with teleaction technologies coming on top of the technology of mere conventional television.

This abrupt transfer of technology, from the building of real-space infrastructures (ports, railway stations, airports) to the control of the real-time environment thanks to interactive teletechnologies (tele-ports), gives new life today to the critical dimension.

Indeed, the question of the real instant of instantaneous teleaction raises once again the philosophical and political problems traditionally associated with the notions of **atopia** and **utopia**, and promotes what is already being referred to as **teletopia**, with all the numerous paradoxes attendant on this, such as:

Meeting at a distance, in other words, **being telepresent**, here and elsewhere, *at the same time,* in this so-called 'real time' which is, however, nothing but a kind of real space-time, since the different events do indeed take *place*, even if that place is in the end the no-place of teletopical techniques (the man–machine interface, the nodes or packet-switching exchanges of teletransmission).

Immediate teleaction, instantaneous telepresence. Thanks to the new practices of television broadcasting or remote transmission, *acting*, the famous teleacting of remote control, is here facilitated by the maximum performance of electromagnetism and by the radioelectric views of what is now called **optoelectronics**, the perceptual faculties of the individual's body being transferred one by one to machines – but also, most recently, to captors, sensors and other microprocessor detectors, capable of making up for the lack of tactility at a distance, *widespread remote control* preparing to take up where *permanent tele-surveillance* left off.

What then becomes critical is not so much the three dimensions of space, but the fourth dimension of time – more precisely, the dimension of the **present** since, as we will see below, 'real time' is not the opposite of 'delayed time', as electronics engineers claim, but only of the 'present'.

Paul Klee hit the nail on the head: 'To define the present in iso-lation is to kill it.' This is what the teletechnologies of real time are doing: they are killing 'present' time by isolating it from its here and now, in favour of a commutative elsewhere that no longer has any-thing to do with our 'concrete presence' in the world, but is the elsewhere of a 'discreet telepresence' that remains a complete mystery.

How can we fail to see how much such radiotechnologies (digital signal, video signal, radio signal) will shortly turn on their heads not only the nature of the human environment, our *territorial body*, but most importantly, the nature of the individual and their *animal body*? For the staking out of the territory with heavy material infrastructure (roads, railroads) is now giving way to control of the immaterial, or practically immaterial, environment (satellites, fibre-optic cables), ending in the *body terminal* of man, of that interactive being who is both transmitter and receiver.

The urbanization of real time is in fact first the urbanization of *one's own body* plugged into various interfaces (keyboard, cathode screen, DataGlove or DataSuit), prostheses that make the super-equipped able-bodied person almost the exact equivalent of the motorized and wired disabled person.

If last century's revolution in transportation saw the emergence and gradual popularization of the dynamic motor vehicle (train, motorbike, car, plane), the current revolution in transmission leads in turn to the innovation of the ultimate vehicle: the static audiovisual vehicle, marking the advent of a behavioural inertia in the sender/receiver that moves us along from the celebrated *retinal persistence* which permits the optical illusion of cinematic projection to the *bodily persistence* of this 'terminal-man'; a prerequisite for the sudden mobilization of the illusion of the world, of a *whole* world, telepresent at each moment, the witness's own body becoming the last urban frontier. Social organization and a kind of conditioning once limited to the space of the city and to the space of the family home finally closing in on the animal body.

This makes it easier to understand the decline in that unit of population, the family, initially extended then nuclearized, that is today becoming a single-parent family, individualism having little to do with the fact of a liberation of values and being more an effect of technological evolution in the development of public and private space, since the more the city expands and spreads its tentacles, the more the family unit dwindles and becomes a minority.

Recent **megalopolitan** hyperconcentration (Mexico City, Tokyo) being itself the result of the increased speed of exchanges, it looks as though we need to reconsider the importance of the notions of **acceleration** and **deceleration** (vector quantities with positive or negative velocities according to the physicists). But we also need to reconsider the less obvious notions of **true velocity** and **virtual velocity** – the speed of that which occurs unexpectedly: a crisis, for instance, an accident – properly to understand the importance of the 'critical transition' of which we are today helpless witnesses.

As we know, speed is not a phenomenon but a relationship between phenomena: in other words, relativity itself. Which is why the constant of the speed of light is so important, not only in physics or astrophysics, but in our daily lives, from the moment we step beyond the transport age into the organization and *electromagnetic conditioning of the territory*.

This is the 'transmission revolution' itself, this control of the environment in real time that has now put paid to traditional development of a real territory.

Speed not only allows us to get around more easily; it enables us above all to see, to hear, to perceive and thus to conceive the present world more intensely. Tomorrow, it will enable us to act at a distance, beyond the human body's sphere of influence and that of its behavioural ergonomics.

How can we fully take in such a situation without enlisting the aid of a new type of interval, **the interval of the light kind** (neutral sign)? The relativistic innovation of this third interval is actually in itself a sort of unremarked cultural revelation.

If the interval of **time** (positive sign) and the interval of **space** (negative sign) have laid out the geography and history of the world through the geometric design of agrarian areas (fragmentation into plots of land) and urban areas (the cadastral system), the organization of calendars and the measurement of time (clocks) have also presided over a vast chronopolitical regulation of human societies. The very recent emergence of an interval of the third type thus signals a sudden qualitative leap, a profound mutation in the relationship between man and his surroundings.

Time (duration) and **space** (extension) are now inconceivable without **light** (limit-speed), the cosmological constant of the **speed of light**, an absolute philosophical contingency that supersedes, in Einstein's wake, the absolute character till then accorded to space and to time by Newton and many others before him.

Since the turn of the century, the absolute limit of the speed of light has *lit up*, so to speak, both space and time. So it is not so much **light** that illuminates things (the object, the subject, the path); it is the constant nature of light's **limit speed** that conditions the perception of duration and of the world's expanse as phenomena.

Listen to a physicist talking about the logic of elementary particles: 'A display is defined by a complete set of observables that commutate.'[1] It would be hard to find a better description of the macroscopic logic of **real-time** technologies than this 'teletopical commutation' – or 'switch-over' – that completes and perfects the till now fundamentally 'topical' nature of the City of Men.

So, politicians, just as much as urbanists, find themselves torn between the permanent requirements of organizing and constructing real space – with its land problems, the geometric and geographic constraints of the centre and the periphery – and the new requirements of managing the real time of immediacy and ubiquity, with its access protocols, its 'data packet transmissions' and its viruses, as well as the chronogeographic constraints of nodes and network interconnection. Long term for the topical and architectonic interval (the building);

short, ultra-short – if not indeed non-existent – term for the **tele-topical** interval (the network).

How do we resolve this dilemma? How do we frame these basically spatio-temporal and relativistic problems?

When we look at all the difficulties faced by world money markets and the disasters of electronic share quotation systems, with the 'Program Trading' being responsible for the acceleration of economic chaos – indeed, for the computer crash of October 1987 and the one narrowly averted in October 1989 – it is pretty clear how fraught the present situation is.

Critical transition then is not an empty term: it masks a true crisis in the temporal dimension of *immediate action*. Following the crisis in 'whole' spatial dimensions and the resultant rise of 'fractional' dimensions, we will soon see a crisis, in short, in the temporal dimension of the present moment.

Since **time-light** (the time of the speed of light) is now used as an absolute standard for immediate action, for instantaneous teleaction, the intensive duration of the 'real moment' now dominates duration, the extensive and relatively controllable time of history – in other words, of that long term that used to encompass past, present and future. This is in the end what we could call a **temporal commutation**, a commutation also related to a sort of **commotion** in present duration, an accident of a so-called 'real' moment that suddenly detaches itself from the place where it happens, from its here and now, and opts for an electronic dazzlement (at once optoelectronic, electroacoustic and electrotactile) in which remote control, this so-called 'tactile telepresence', will complete the task of the old telesurveillance of whatever stays at a distance, out of our reach.

According to Epicurus, *time is the accident to end all accidents.* If this is so, then with the teletechnologies of general interactivity we are entering the age of the **accident of the present**, this overhyped remote telepresence being only ever the sudden catastrophe of the reality of the present moment that is our sole entry into duration –

but also, as everyone knows since Einstein, our entry into the expanse of the real world.

After this, the real time of telecommunications would no longer refer only to delayed time, but also to an *ultra-chronology*. Hence my repeatedly reiterated proposal to round off the chronological (before, during, after) with the **dromological** or, if you like, the **chrono-scopic** (underexposed, exposed, overexposed). Indeed, the interval of the light kind (the interface) taking over in future from those of space and time, the notion of exposure in turn takes over from the notion of succession in the measurement of present duration as well as from the notion of extension in the immediate physical expanse.

The exposure speed of time-light might therefore enable us to rein-terpret the 'present', this 'real instant' which is, let's not forget, the space-time of a perfectly real action helped along by the feats of elec-tronics and shortly of photonics – that is, by the limit capabilities of electromagnetic radiation and of the light quantum, that frontier-post of access to the reality of the perceptible world (note here the light cone – or illuminating pencil – used by astrophysicists).

The question today posed by teletopical technologies is thus a major one for the planner, since the urbanization of real time per-mitted by the recent transmission revolution leads to a radical reversal in the order of the movement of displacement and of physical trans-portation. In fact, if operating remotely allows gradual elimination of the material infrastructures rigging out the territory in favour of the fundamentally immaterial wave trains of telesurveillance and instan-taneous remote control, this is because the **journey** and its components are undergoing a veritable mutation-commutation. Where physical displacement from one point to another once sup-posed departure, a journey and arrival, the transport revolution of last century had already quietly begun to eliminate delay and change the nature of travel itself, arrival at one's destination remaining, however, a 'limited arrival' due to the very time it took to get there.

Currently, with the instantaneous broadcasting revolution, we are seeing the beginnings of a *'generalized arrival'* whereby everything arrives without having to leave, the nineteenth century's elimination of the journey (that is, of the space interval and of time) combining with the abolition of *departure* at the end of the twentieth, the journey thereby losing its successive components and being overtaken by *arrival* alone.

A **general arrival** that explains the unheard-of innovation today of the static vehicle, a vehicle not only audiovisual but also tactile and interactive (radioactive, optoactive, interactive).

One such static vehicle is the 'DataSuit', invented by the American Scott Fisher while he was working for NASA on the development of a human body device that would be capable of transferring actions and sensations by means of an array of sensor-effectors. In other words, capable of producing *presence at a distance*, and this no matter what the distance, since the NASA project was supposed to allow total telemanipulation of a *robotic double* on the surface of planet Mars, thus achieving the individual's effective telepresence in two places at the same time, a split in the personality of the manipulator, whose 'vehicle' was to be this instantaneous interactive vector.

To cite another of Paul Klee's premonitory sayings: 'The viewer's main activity is temporal.'

What can we say about the interactivity of the *teleoperator* other than that, for such a person (at the human–robot interface), as for the now time-honoured *televiewer*, activity is not so much spatial as temporal?

Doomed to inertia, the interactive being transfers his natural capacities for movement and displacement to probes and scanners which instantaneously inform him about a remote reality, to the detriment of his own faculties of apprehension of the real, after the example of the para- or quadriplegic who can guide by remote control – *teleguide* – his environment, his abode, which is a model of that home automation, of those 'Smart Houses' that respond to our every whim. Having been first *mobile*, then *motorized*, man will thus become *motile*, deliberately limiting his body's area of influence to a few gestures, a few impulses, like channel-surfing.

This critical situation is no different from that experienced by any number of spastics who thus become by force of circumstance – the critical force of the circumstance of technology – models of the new man, of that inhabitant of the future teletopical city, the **metacity** of a social deregulation the transpolitical aspect of which already shows up, here and there, in a number of major accidents or minor incidents, mostly remaining as yet unexplained.

How can we get a purchase on this transitional situation, this 'phase transition', as the physicists would say?

Here is a rather ancient piece of philosophical analysis from Nicholas of Cusa: 'The accident ceases to exist when the substance is removed, and its ceasing to exist in that instance is due to the fact that to inhere is of the nature of an accident and that its subsistence is the subsistence of the substance. Yet it cannot be said that an accident is nothing. . . . An accident gives something to a substance . . . ; in fact, an accident gives so much to a substance that, although the accident had its being from the substance, *the substance cannot exist without any accident*.'[2]

Today, as we have seen, the problem of the accident has shifted from the space of matter to the time of light.

The accident is, first, an *accident of transfer* of the limit-speed of electromagnetic waves, a speed that now allows us not only to hear and see at a distance, as we were already able to do with the telephone, radio or television, but actually to act at a distance. Hence the necessity of the third type of interval (neutral sign) to try and grasp the *place of the no-place* of a teleaction that is no longer the same as the here and now of immediate action.

So interactivity's *accident of transfer* opens not only on to the *technology transfer* between delayed time communication and real-time commutation, but more particularly on to a political transfer that undermines precisely those notions that lie at the heart of our age: the notion of *service* and the notion of *public*.

What, indeed, is left of the notion of *service* when you are automatically controlled? Similarly, what is left of the notion of *public* when the (real-time) public image prevails over public space?

Already the notion of public transport is gradually giving way to the idea of a *transit corridor*, the continuous prevailing over the discontinuous. What can one say about the wired household of electronic domesticity, with houses that have computers wired into them, controlling the house systems, or of the smart building, indeed the intelligent and interactive city such as Kawasaki? The crisis in the notion of physical dimensions thus hits politics and the administration of public services head on in attacking what was once geopolitics.

If the classic interval is giving way to the interface, politics in turn is shifting within exclusively *present time*. The question is then no longer one of the **global** versus the **local**, or of the **transnational** versus the **national**. It is, first and foremost, a question of the sudden temporal switch in which not only inside and outside disappear, the expanse of the political territory, but also the before and after of its duration, of its history; all that remains is a **real instant** over which, in the end, no one has any control. For proof of this, one need look no further than the inextricable mess geostrategy is in thanks to the impossibility of clearly distinguishing now between offensive and defensive – instantaneous, multipolar strategy now being deployed in 'preemptive' strikes, as they say in the military.

And so the age-old *tyranny of distance* between beings geographically distributed in different places is gradually yielding to the *tyranny of real time* which is not the exclusive concern of travel agents, as optimists claim, but a special concern of the employment agency, since the greater the speed of exchanges, the more unemployment spreads and becomes mass unemployment.

Redundancy of man's muscular strength in favour of the 'machine tool' from the nineteenth century on. Now redundancy, permanent unemployment, of his memory and his consciousness, with the recent boom in computers, in 'transfer machines', and the automation of postindustrial production combining with the automation of perception, and finally with computer-aided design, enabled by the software market, ahead of the coming of the artificial intelligence market.

To gain real time over delayed time is thus to commit to a quick way of physically eliminating the object and the subject and exclusively promoting the journey. But a journey without a trajectory and hence fundamentally uncontrollable.

The real-time interface then once and for all replaces the interval that once constituted and organized the history and geography of human societies, winding up in a true culture of the paradox in which everything arrives not only without needing physically to move from one place to another but, more particularly, without having to leave.

Surely we cannot fail to foresee the future conditioning of the human environment behind this critical transition.

If last century's transport revolution already brought about a mutation in urban territory throughout the continent, the current revolution in (interactive) transmission is in turn provoking a commutation in the urban environment whereby the image prevails over the thing it is an image of; what was once a city becoming little by little a paradoxical agglomeration, relationships of immediate proximity giving way to remote interrelationships.

The paradoxes of acceleration are indeed numerous and discon-
certing, in particular, the foremost among them: getting closer to the
'distant' takes you away proportionally from the 'near' (and dear) –
the friend, the relative, the neighbour – thus making strangers, if not
actual enemies, of all who are close at hand, whether they be family,
workmates or neighbourhood acquaintances. This inversion of social
practices, already evident in the development of communication
equipment (ports, stations, airports), is further reinforced, radical-
ized, by the new telecommunications equipment (teleports).

Once more we are seeing a reversal in trends: where the motorization
of transport and information once caused a *general mobilization* of
populations, swept up into the exodus of work and then of leisure,
instantaneous transmission tools cause the reverse: *a growing inertia;*
television and especially remote control action no longer requiring
people to be mobile, but merely to be mobile on the spot.

Home shopping, working from home, online apartments and
buildings: 'cocooning', as they say. The urbanization of real space is
thus being overtaken by this urbanization of real time which is, at the
end of the day, the urbanization of the actual body of the city dweller,
this *citizen-terminal* soon to be decked out to the eyeballs with interactive prostheses based on the pathological model of the 'spastic',
wired to control his/her domestic environment without having
physically to stir: the catastrophic figure of an individual who has lost
the capacity for immediate intervention along with natural motricity
and who abandons himself, for want of anything better, to the capabilities of captors, sensors and other remote control scanners that
turn him into a being controlled by the machine with which, they
say, he talks.[3]

Service or servitude, that is the question. The old public services are
in danger of being replaced by a domestic enslavement whose crown-
ing glory would surely be home automation. Achieving a domiciliary

inertia, the widespread use of techniques of *environmental control* will end in behavioural isolation, in intensifying the insularity that has always threatened the town, the difference between the (separate) 'block' and the (segregated) 'ghetto' remaining precarious.

Curiously, papers given at an international symposium on disability recently held in Dunkirk in many ways echoed the critical situation evoked here, as though recent technological and economic imperatives to produce *continuity and networks*, wherever *discontinuities* still exist, failed to distinguish between the various kinds of urban mobility. Hence the above-mentioned idea of scrapping the notion of public transport and opting instead for the broader one of transit corridors.

This was François Mitterrand's noble conclusion to the Dunkirk conference: 'Cities must adapt to their citizens and not the other way round. Let's open up the city to the physically challenged. I ask that an overall policy on the disabled be a firm axis of Europe as a social institution.'

Though none of us would dispute the inalienable right of the disabled to live the same way as everyone else, and therefore with everyone else, it is none the less revealing to note the convergences that now exist between the reduced mobility of the well-equipped disabled person and the growing inertia of the overequipped able-bodied person, as though the transmission revolution always yielded an identical result, no matter what the bodily condition of the patient, this **terminal citizen** of a teletopical City that is going up faster and faster.

At the end of the century, there will not be much left of the expanse of a planet that is not only polluted but also shrunk, reduced to nothing, by the teletechnologies of generalized interactivity.

THE PERSPECTIVE OF
REAL TIME

'Eliminating distance kills.'
René Char

Alongside air pollution, water pollution and the like, there exists an unnoticed phenomenon of pollution of the world's dimensions that I propose to call **dromospheric** – from *dromos*: a race, running.

Contamination has in fact spread further than the elements, natural substances, air, water, fauna and flora it attacks – as far as the space-time of our planet. Gradually reduced to nothing by the various tools of transport and instantaneous communication, the geophysical environment is undergoing an alarming diminishing of its 'depth of field' and this is degrading man's relationship with his environment. *The optical density of the landscape* is rapidly evaporating, producing confusion between the *apparent* horizon, which is the backdrop of all action, and the *deep* horizon of our collective imagination; and so one last horizon of visibility comes into view, *the transapparent horizon*, a product of the optical (optoelectronic and acoustic) magnification of man's natural domain.

So, there exists a hidden dimension to the communications revolution, one that affects duration, the lived time of our society.

This is where, as I see it, a certain 'ecology' comes up against its limits, its theoretical narrowness, in depriving itself of some approach to the regimes of temporality associated with the various 'ecosystems', in particular those that stem from the industrial and postindustrial technosphere.

As a science of the finite world, the science of the human environment deprives itself deliberately, it would seem, of its connection with psychological time. Following in the footsteps of that 'universal' science denounced by Edmund Husserl, ecology does not really question the man–machine dialogue, the close correlation between different regimes of perception and the collective practices of communication and telecommunication.[1]

In a word, ecology as a discipline does not sufficiently register the impact of *machine time* on the environment, leaving this concern to ergonomics, to economics, indeed to 'politics' alone.

Everywhere you turn there is the same disastrous lack of understanding of the relativistic nature of the activities of modern industrial man. This is where **dromology** comes in. Unless we treat ecology simply as public management of profits and losses in the substances and stocks that make up the human environment, it can no longer effectively make headway without also making sense of the temporal economy of interactive activities and their rapid mutations.

If, as Charles Péguy claimed, *there is no history, but only a public duration*, a collective lifespan, the rhythm and speed peculiar to the world event ought to give rise not only to a 'true sociology', as the poet suggested, but also to an authentic 'public dromology'. Bear in mind that the truth of a phenomenon is always limited by the speed with which it emerges.

Now let us return to the probable source of this ignorance about public rhythmics, the pace of public life.

On a constricted planet that is becoming just one vast floor, the lack of collective resentment over dromospheric pollution stems from our forgetting *the essence of the path, the journey*. In spite of recent studies and debates on seclusion and its hardships affecting this or that group of people deprived of their freedom of movement – totalitarian or penal regimes, blockades, states of siege and so on – it seems we are still incapable of seriously entertaining this *question of the path*, except in the realms of mechanics, ballistics or astronomy.

Objectivity, subjectivity, certainly, but never *trajectivity*.

Despite the great anthropological issue of nomadism and of sedentariness that explains the birth of the city-state as a major political form in history, there is little understanding of the vectorial nature of the transhumant species that we are, of our chorography. Between the subjective and the objective it seems we have no room for the 'trajective', that being of movement from here to there, from one to the other, without which we will never achieve a profound understanding of the various regimes of perception of the world that have succeeded each other throughout the ages – regimes of visibility of appearances related to the history of techniques and modalities of displacement, long-distance communications, the nature of the speed of movement in transport and transmission entailing a transmutation in the 'depth of field' and so in the optical density of the human environment, and not just an evolution in systems of migration or of populating this or that region of the globe.[2]

Today we are confronted with the problematic of the *residual abundance* of the world's expanse in the face of ultra-powerful communication and telecommunication tools: the limit speed of electromagnetic radiation on the one hand and, on the other, the restriction, the drastic reduction of the extent of this geophysical 'vast floor' through the effects of subsonic, supersonic and soon hypersonic transport.

As the physicist, Zhao Fusan, recently explained: 'Contemporary travellers find the world less and less exotic; they are wrong, though, if they think it is becoming uniform.'

This is the end of the outside world. The whole world suddenly becomes endotic. And such an end implies forgetting spatial exteriority as much as temporal exteriority ('no future') and opting exclusively for the 'present' instant, the real instant of instantaneous telecommunications.

When are we going to see legal sanctions, a speed limit, imposed not because of the probability of a road accident but because of the danger of exhausting temporal distances and so of the threat of inertia – in other words, of parking accidents?

'For what doth it profit a man if he gain the whole world but lose his only soul?' Let's not forget that *to gain* also means *to reach*, to get to, as much as to conquer or possess. Losing one's soul, *anima*, means losing the very being of movement.

Historically, we thus find ourselves faced with a sort of great divide in knowing how to *be in the world*: on the one hand, there is the original nomad for whom the *journey*, the being's trajectory, are dominant. On the other, there is the sedentary man for whom *subject* and *object* prevail, movement towards the immovable, the inert, characterizing the sedentary urban 'civilian' in contrast to the 'warrior' nomad.

A movement that is today intensifying due to remote control and long-distance telepresence technologies that will soon land us in the ultimate state of sedentariness where real-time environmental control will take over from the development of the real space of the territory.

Terminal – and final – *sedentarization*; a practical consequence of the emergence of a third and final horizon of indirect visibility (after the apparent and deep horizon): a *transapparent horizon* spawned by telecommunications, that opens up the incredible possibility of a 'civilization of forgetting', a *live* (live-coverage) society that has no future and no past, since it has no extension and no duration, a society intensely present here and there at once – in other words, *telepresent to the whole world.*

Loss of the traveller's tale and, with it, the possibility of some kind of interpretation, which will be coupled with a sharp loss of memory, or rather, with the flourishing of a paradoxical *immediate memory* linked to the all-powerful nature of the image. A *real-time image* no longer offering concrete (explicit) information but discreet (implicit) information, a sort of illumination of the reality of the facts.

So, after the *line* of the visible horizon, the original skyline of the landscape of the world, the *square* horizon of the screen (third horizon of visibility) will emerge as a bug in the memory of the second horizon – that deep horizon of our memory of places responsible for our orientation in the world – causing confusion of near and far, of inside and outside, disorders in common perception that will gravely affect the way we think.

While the topical City was once constructed around the 'gate' and the 'port', the teletopical *metacity* is now reconstructed around the 'window' and the teleport, that is to say, around the screen and the time slot.

No more delay, *no more relief*, volume is no longer the reality of things. This is now concealed in the flatness of figures. Right here and now, life-size is no longer the yardstick of the real. The real is hidden in the reduction of images on the screen. Like a woman worried about putting on weight, being overweight, reality seems to apologize for having a relief, any kind of thickness.

If the *interval* becomes thin, 'infra-thin', in suddenly turning into an *interface*, things and objects perceived also become infra-thin and lose their weight, their bulk.

With the 'law of (electromagnetic) proximity', the far prevails over the near and figures without density prevail over things within reach. The tree in leaf *perceived at a standstill* is no longer the tree of record of the vegetal realm, but just whatever old tree flashes past in the confusion of stroboscopic perception.

'If anyone thinks I paint too fast, they are watching me too fast,' Van Gogh wrote. Already, the classic photograph is no more than a *freeze frame*. With the decline in volumes and in the expanse of landscapes, reality becomes sequential and cinematic unfolding finally gets the jump on whatever is static and on the strength of materials.

It has often been said that vertigo was caused by looking at vertical lines converging on a point. Might the real-space perspective of the Italian Renaissance then be an early form of vertigo arising from the visible horizon, *a horizontal vertigo* caused by a time freeze in the intersection of vanishing lines?

In an important text of 1947, Giulio Carlo Argan wrote: 'The principle of intersection was thus applied to time before being applied to space – unless this new conception of space is, quite simply, the result of the sudden arresting of time.'[3]

Might the famous perspectivist relief of the Quattrocento thus have been just *giddiness* brought on by the time freeze in the real instant of the vanishing-point?

Might the inertia of this **punctum** at the intersection of vanishing lines thus be at the root of such a perspective of real space?

A dominant perspective for only a little while longer. *Relief is the very soul of painting*, wrote Leonardo da Vinci. We might also recall the debate between Auguste Rodin and Paul Gsell about the veracity of the snapshot, the sculptor declaring: 'No, it is art that tells the truth and photography that lies, *for in reality time does not stand still.*'[4]

The kind of time in question here is chronological time, time that does not stand still, that flows continually, ordinary linear time. Now, what the technology of photosensitivity introduced and Rodin had not yet noticed, is that the definition of photographic time was no longer the same as time passing, but essentially a kind of time that gets exposed, that 'breaks the surface' – surfaces; and this exposure time then succeeds the classic time of succession. The time of the sudden *take* is accordingly, from the beginning, **time-light**.

The exposure time of the photographic plate is thus simply the exposure of time, of the space-time of its photosensitive matter, to the light of speed, that is, ultimately, to the frequency of the photon carrier wave. So what the sculptor fails to notice is that only the *surface* of the negative freezes the time of the representation of movement.

With the instant photoprint enabling invention of the cinematographic sequence, *time will not stand still again*. The film strip, the film reel, and later, the *real-time* video cassette of non-stop telesurveillance will all illustrate the incredible innovation of a continuous *time-light* – in other words, the greatest scientific invention since fire, the invention of an indirect light that takes over from the direct light of the sun or of electricity, just as electricity once took over from daylight.

These days, the screen of real-time televised broadcasts is no longer a monochromatic filter like the one familiar to photographers which lets through a single colour only of the spectrum, but a *monochronic* filter which allows a glimpse only of the present. An *intensive present*, spawned by the limit-speed of electromagnetic waves and no longer registered in chronological time – past-present-future – but in chronoscopic time: underexposed-exposed-overexposed.

The real-time perspective of video's *transapparent* horizon thus exists only through the inertia of the present moment, where once the perspective of the real space of the Quattrocento's *apparent* horizon subsisted only through a blackout, a time freeze, a dizzy spell afflicting the heart of this body of which Merleau-Ponty once told us: 'Our own body is in the world as the heart is in the organism: it keeps the visible spectacle constantly alive, it breathes life into it and sustains it inwardly, and with it forms a system.'[5]

'Time freeze' in the intersection of the vanishing lines of perspective geometry. Time freeze in photographic instantaneity. Time freeze, finally, in the real instant of the live television broadcast. It does indeed look as though the world's relief (or, more exactly, its high definition) is merely the effect of an imperceptible *fixing of the present*. A pyknoleptic fixedness, infinitesimal lack of duration without which the spectacle of the visible would quite simply not take place.

Rather as light from distant stars is deflected by an imposing mass, favouring the illusion of gravitational optics, our perception of depth might well be a kind of visual plunge, comparable to the fall of bodies in the law of universal gravitation. If so, the perspective of the real space of the Quattrocento would have been early scientific evidence of this. In fact, from that moment in history, optics becomes kinematic. Galileo was to supply proof of this in the face of all opposition. With the Renaissance perspectivists, we 'fall' into the volume of the visible spectacle as though by the force of gravity; literally, the world *opens up* before us. Much later, physiologists will discover that *the faster you move from one place to another*, the *further ahead* your eyes adapt. From then on, the old 'vanishing lines vertigo' is coupled with the projection involved in *focusing* one's eyes.

To illustrate this sudden magnification of vision as a result of an increase in speed, here is the tale of a parachutist, a free fall specialist:

'Eyeballing consists in visually assessing the distance between you and the ground the whole time you are falling. You evaluate your height and work out the exact moment you need to open your parachute based on a *dynamic visual impression*. When you are flying in a plane at an altitude of 600 metres, you don't have anything like the visual impression you have when you clear this altitude in a high-speed vertical fall. When you are at 2,000 metres, you can't see the ground approaching. But when you reach the 800 to 600 metre mark, you start to see it "coming". The sensation becomes scary pretty quickly because of ground rush, the ground rushing up at you. The apparent diameter of objects increases faster and faster and you suddenly have the feeling you are not seeing them getting closer but seeing them move apart suddenly, as though *the ground were splitting open*.'[6]

This account is invaluable as it illustrates in a truly gravitational way the dizziness induced by perspective, its apparent weightiness. To this 'eyeballer', perspective geometry appears for what it has never ceased to be: *a headlong rush of perception* in which the very rapidity of free fall reveals the fractal nature of vision that results from high-speed eye adaptation.

In this experience, at a certain distance, at a certain moment, the ground no longer approaches, but parts and splits open, going suddenly from a 'whole' dimension *with no receding lines*, to a 'fractional' dimension in which the visible spectacle gapes open.

Even though it hardly seems humanly possible to take this eye-balling process to its limit, it is already clear that vision here depends closely on gravity.

The *headlong* perspective is no longer so much that of the real – vertical or horizontal – space of the Italian geometers; it is first and foremost that of the real time of falling bodies. The horizon of visibility of the 'faller' prior to being smashed to smithereens depends essentially on the speed at which his eyes adapt, focusing and an imperceptible time freeze depending on the mass of his body itself. *The path's being* defines *the subject's perception* through *the object's mass*. The falling body suddenly becomes *the body of the fall*.

If isolation distorts perspective, what is isolated here is the instant of hurtling down into earth's gravitational field. Perspective is not so much bound up with space any more but with the time remaining, this 'fall time' that depends closely on gravity.

Suddenly all geometric dimensions connect: at first the ground seems **to come up**, then **to open up**; the arrival of a *surface* is followed by the spreading of the vanishing lines of a *volume*, anticipating flattening at the *point* of impact; the *line* is the person, the being on the path of a fall free from all resistance.[7]

A perilous exercise if ever there was one, just to test dynamic visual impressions or, in other words, **kinematic optics**.

Today, curiously, a growing number of adepts share the attraction of the void and the extreme sensations it offers, through bungee jumping, sky surfing, BASE jumping, and so on, as though the accelerated perspective had already won out over the passive perspective of the perspectivists. Suicidal experiments on the inertia of a body pulled by its mass without the aid of any support other than air, in the relative wind of a dizzying displacement, with no other aim than that of experiencing the heaviness of the body.

On earth, *escape velocity* is around 11,200 metres a second. Below this acceleration, all speeds are affected by earth's gravity well, including the speed at which we see things. With centrifugal and centripetal forces on the one hand, and resistance to forward motion on the other, every movement of physical displacement, whether horizontal or vertical, thus depends on the force of gravity at the surface of the globe.

Given this, surely we should try and evaluate the interaction between gravity and our perception of the world's landscape.

If light is deflected close to an extended mass by universal gravity, that same attractive force (whose speed, we should remember, is the same as the speed of electromagnetic waves) will surely influence the world's appearances, that spectacle of the visible Merleau-Ponty spoke of. How, indeed, can we picture any spatial or atmospheric perspective once we have lost 'high' and 'low' as referents? And the same goes for the split between 'near' and 'far', once we have lost resistance to forward motion.

Astronauts have already carried out full-scale experiments on sensory disorders and problems in orientation caused by weightlessness. We cannot today acknowledge this fact without immediately trying to reinterpret geometric perspective *à l'italienne*.

If from the Quattrocento onwards the visible spectacle gapes open in the intersection of vanishing lines, this is due to the force of earth's gravity and not solely to some convergence effect, the strabismus of a metrics of tangible appearances so dear to the Italian artists. The organization of the new apparent horizon already depended on time, on that *time freeze* of the vanishing-point so masterfully analysed by Argan. Today, the reorganization of appearances that is under way and the approaching emergence of a last horizon of visibility constituted by the transparency of appearances *instantaneously* transmitted at a distance, can only be achieved by overcoming the constraint imposed by the force of gravity.

Unlike the real-space perspective of geometry, the perspective of real time is no longer constrained by terrestrial weightiness; the *transapparent* horizon of the live telecast screen escapes gravitation by basing itself on the very speed of light.

If, in keeping with the images it instantaneously transmits, the screen has optical and geometric properties that suggest a window or the frame of a painting, the constitution of its *videoscopic information* depends in particular on an acceleration not limited by the force of gravity at 300,000 kilometres per second.

The 'time freeze' in the intersection of the Quattrocento's receding lines then gives way to video's imperceptible freeze frame (note here the quest for the high-definition image). So the sole *freeze* is that of a pyknoleptic absence of the *present moment*; with the equally imperceptible freeze of the televiewer's attention span – which saves him from having to hallucinate an unending stream. 'We just have to accept it,' as Einstein said, '*there is no fixed point in space*'. There is only the inertia of the real moment which gives shape to the *living present* – a psychological timespan without which no apprehension of the world would exist, no worldly landscape.

But let us get back to the origins of this last form of pollution, *dromospheric pollution*.

If the hegemonic influence of technological culture is spreading and taking over our planet, entailing an apparent territorial expansion, this development has a hidden side to it.

As Samuel Beckett remarked: 'Art tends not to make bigger but to shrink.'

The very boom in vehicles and sundry vectors of progression entails an imperceptible telluric contraction of the world and of our immediate environment. The imperceptible 'time freeze' in the intersection of perspective's vanishing lines then gives way to a 'world freeze', that is to say, to an imperceptible withholding of the world's extension and of its regional diversity. The vertigo of real space was caused by the sight – eyeballing – of vanishing vertical lines, a perspective accelerated by anticipation of falling into the void. But these days, for the traveller-voyeur in the fast lane and especially for the televiewer, the vertigo of real time is brought on by inertia, the *on-the-spot contraction* of the passenger-onlooker's body.

The speed of the new optoelectronic and electroacoustic milieu becomes the final **void** (the void of the quick), a vacuum that no longer depends on the interval between places or things and so on the world's very extension, but on the interface of an instantaneous transmission of remote appearances, on a geographic and geometric retention in which all volume, all relief vanish.

This is the crisis in, or, more precisely, the accident of, the *optical density* of the visible spectacle and the landscape. As Théodore Monod wrote: 'Nothing is more depressing than already seeing from the place you are leaving the one you will reach later that day or the next.'

Loss of sight or, rather, 'loss of ground' in a new kind of fall that is also a form of pollution of expanse, of that 'art of the journey' practised by the nomad, a peculiar form of vertigo brought on by the depth of field of the apparent horizon of the spectacle of the world.

With the contemporary sedentary type of the great metropolis, this on-the-spot contraction not only affects the transit zone and the sphere of productive activity as before. First and foremost, it attacks the body of the able-bodied person, equipped to the eyeballs with interactive prostheses, who is now modelled on the disabled person equipped to control his environment without physically shifting.

So dromospheric pollution is pollution that attacks the liveliness of the *subject* and the mobility of the *object* by atrophying the *journey* to the point where it becomes needless. A major handicap, resulting both from *the loss of the locomotive body* of the passenger, the tele-viewer, and from the loss of that solid ground, of that vast floor, identity's adventure playground of being in the world.

Optics on a Grand Scale

'The better telescopes become the more stars there will be.'
Gustave Flaubert

What can we say about the splitting of sight, the emergence of a second optics, the optics that now makes **teleconferencing** between Tokyo and Paris possible?

A few souls were already talking about *a hole in space* some years ago; others, more recently, have been talking about *a hole in time*, the real time of the instantaneous transmission of historic events and, in particular, the Gulf War. This semantic vacillation seems characteristic of the perceptual disorder now afflicting our society, confronted as it is by the progress in teletechnologies and the dwindling importance of geometric optics, the *passive optics* of the space of matter (glass, water, air) which, in the end, only covers man's immediate proximity.

We will call this *small-scale optics* and keep the term '*large-scale optics*' for physical optics, the **active optics** of the time of the speed of light, since such an optics disregards the traditional notion of a horizon.

It is also clear that the optoelectronics of video signal carrier waves brings us to the question of the digitization of the video signal. Everyone agrees on the importance of this signal not only in the area of astronomic observation, with the feats of so-called 'adaptive' optics, but especially in the recent implementation of *virtual reality spaces*.

Since optics is the branch of physics that deals with the properties of light and so with visualization phenomena, the split in sight is now saddled with the split in light itself: not just the old split between *natural* light (sun) and *artificial* light (electricity), but the current split between *direct* light (sun and electricity) and *indirect* light (video-surveillance) that results from the interaction of real time, optical phenomena and electronics. Whence the term '**optoelectronics**'.

All this leads us at this juncture to speak not solely of the extension and duration of the space of matter, as the philosophers of the classical age did, but also of the *optical density* of the time of light and of its 'optoelectronic' amplification. This means chucking out the geometric perspective of the Italian Renaissance and replacing it with an electronic perspective: that of real-time emission and instantaneous reception of audio-video signals.

So, given the new impetus recently given to the geometric optics of light rays by the physical optics of the electromagnetic propagation of particles carrying sight and hearing, we are seeing the emergence of a final type of transparence: *the transparence of appearances transmitted long-distance instantaneously.* A **trans-appearance** which then completes (finishes off, so to speak) the natural trans-appearance of the earth's atmosphere, producing in the process a sort of stereoscopic intensification of tangible appearances, of representation of the world and so, indirectly, of aesthetics itself. The aesthetics of the appearance of objects or people standing out against the *apparent horizon* of classical perspective's unity of time and place is then taken over by the aesthetics of the disappearance of far-off characters looming up against the lack of horizon of a cathode screen where unity of time wins out over the unity of the place of encounter. The *real-time perspective* of large-scale optics once and for all outstrips the small-scale optics of *the perspective of real space*, the vanishing-point of focusing light rays surrendering its primacy to the vanishing of all the points (pixels) of the televised image.

★

From that moment, the *direct* transparence of space that enables each of us to perceive our immediate neighbours is completed by the *indirect* transparence of the speed-time of the electromagnetic waves that transmit our images and our voices and tomorrow, no doubt, our reciprocal actions, thanks to the DataSuit that will pave the way for shared teleaction, on top of mere television or teleaudition.

But, before broaching the issue of our future **tele-existence**, we might take another look at this electromagnetic *large-scale optics* that now enables us to meet at a distance, at opposite ends of the globe. The direct lighting of the day star that breaks up the activity of our years into distinct days is now supplemented by indirect lighting, the 'light' of a technology that promotes a sort of personality split in time between the real time of our *immediate activities* – in which we act both here *and* now – and the real time of a *media interactivity* that privileges the 'now' of the time slot of the televised broadcast to the detriment of the 'here', that is to say, of the space of the meeting place. In the manner of a teleconference that takes place thanks to a satellite, but which does so, paradoxically, nowhere in the world.

How can we really live if there is no more *here* and if everything is *now*? How can we survive the instantaneous telescoping of a reality that has become ubiquitous, breaking up into two orders of time, each as real as the other: that of presence here and now, and that of a telepresence at a distance, beyond the horizon of tangible appearances?

How can we rationally manage the split, not only between virtual and actual realities but, more to the point, between the *apparent* horizon and the *transapparent* horizon of a screen that suddenly opens up a kind of temporal window for us to interact elsewhere, often a long way away?

Unless, like Marvin Minsky, we deny the importance of 'analogue' optics and so of the horizon of appearances, we must now absolutely question the **stereoscopic** nature not only of the 'relief of appearances' and of the third dimension of space, but above all of the fourth dimension, the *temporal relief* brought about this time by the split between spatial and temporal proximities, the relief of a world in future overexposed to the optoelectronic amplification of its depth of field.

'Presence is only presence at a distance and this distance is absolute, that is, irreducible,' wrote Maurice Blanchot.

Today, when the notion of 'distance' has given way in physics to the notion of an instantaneous transmitting 'power', physical optics winds up in 'a fluctuation of appearances' in which distance is no longer, as the poet hoped, presence's depth, but merely its flickering. The space interval (negative sign) and the time interval (positive sign) having not long ago bowed down before the neutral-sign interval of the *light-speed* of information carrier waves, we might now move on to the problems posed by the innovation of 'signal digitization' (audio, video and tactile): technology enabling not only the implementation of the *representation* of tangible reality, as previously with the aesthetics of appearance, but also its untimely *presentation* thanks to the scanners, probes and other remote sensors of what is known as *telepresence*.

We might recall in passing that there is no true presence in the World – in one's own world of sense experience – other than through the intermediary of the egocentration of a *living present*; in other words, through the existence of one's own body living in the here and now.

Whether the cognitivists like it or not, the question posed by intermittent 'long-distance telepresence' thus introduces a series of questions analogous to those posed in physics by Planck's famous *length*: when extreme spatial distancing suddenly gives way to the extreme proximity of the real time of exchange, *there still remains an irreducible gap*.

Despite the lack of interval due to the nonexistence of the real space of encounter, the neutral-sign interface of electromagnetic radiation enabling telecommunication to occur rules out the usual confusion of the 'here and now', the instantaneity of interactivity never actually managing to eliminate the difference between the act and remote action.

The same goes for shared *tele-existence*, no matter what the degree of proximity of teleoperators gathered at a distance.

So, alongside use of the helmet or head-mounted display (HMD) and the sensor-lined bodysuit (DataSuit) in the realm of virtual space (**cyberspace**), both of which induce an initial personality split in time between *real* and *virtual*, the same kind of *electroergonomic* equipment is also used in a practice relating to the actual space of long-distance exchanges: the practice of the *teleoperator* (or telemanipulator), thanks to recent advances in *interactive tactile telepresence* whereby the 'high relief' of touch at a distance now rounds off 'high fidelity' in sound and 'high definition' in visuals.

Hence the impending emergence of a purely 'temporal' volume and the concomitant *advent of the prospect of real-time touching*, which will turn the perspectivists' classic visualization and, consequently, next century's vision of the world on its head.

Note also that *large-scale physical optics* is no longer concerned solely with visual scope; it now involves every facet of perception of tangible appearances – including the sense of touch. *This is because time, the real time of the third light-type interval of electromagnetic radiation*, wins out once and for all over the real space of matter, over the *extension and duration* of the substances that make up the narrow human environment.

Thanks to so-called 'force-feedback' technologies, to feedback from the **teletact** DataGlove recently put on the market and, in the near future, to the full teletactile bodysuit in which touch, impact will involve the whole body, we will see industrial production of a personality split, an instantaneous cloning of living man, the technological re-creation of one of our most ancient myths: the myth of the **double**, of an electroergonomic double whose presence is spectral – another way of saying a ghost or the living dead.

It really is impossible not to evoke the theatre intrinsic to this kind of novel technology.

The trauma of birth does not just affect the infant, the subject alone, it also affects the object, the instrument that comes into being. So we need to try and unearth 'the original accident' specific to this kind of technological innovation. Unless we are deliberately forgetting *the invention of the shipwreck* in the invention of the ship or *the rail accident* in the advent of the train, we need to examine the hidden face of new technologies, before that face reveals itself in spite of us.

Already, *viral contamination* offers an initial response to the question of the downside of electronic circuits, but another area of research beckons: the area of *ecological pollution*. The pollution not only of air, water and other 'substances', but also the unperceived pollution of 'distances', this **dromospheric** contamination of time distances that reduces to nothing, or next to nothing, the expanse of a constricted planet hanging in the vacuum of space.

After all the attention we earthlings have legitimately paid to the pollution of **nature**, surely we should be equally anxious to study this pollution of the **life-size** (*grandeur-nature*) triggered by the growth of real-time technologies.

While geometric **small-scale optics** enabled us to perceive, and so to conceive, our own world as 'extension' and 'duration', that is to say, as a geographic quantity, thanks to the very vastness of the real space of appearances, physical **large-scale optics** conversely now dissolves the scale of the human environment.

With the real-time transmitting and receiving power of the various signals alienating the nature of time distances, the active optics of electromagnetic waves *exploits* the depth of field, the very reality of our own world to the point of reducing it to nothing, or next to nothing, thereby leading to a catastrophic sense of incarceration now that humanity is literally deprived of horizon.

Where the *passive* small-scale optics of the space of matter – air, water, lens glass – was happy just to serve up the **great world** of appearances for our contemplation, the *active* large-scale optics of the time of the speed of light opens, beyond any horizon, on to flickering perception of the **small world** of the transparence of waves bearing various signals: a 'transappearance' that eliminates the normal boundary of the horizon line, exclusively promoting the screen frame, 'the square horizon' of a kind of split-perspective reality. A **stereo-reality** in which the 'high notes' and 'low notes' of the sound landscape of high-fidelity acoustics will be replaced, on one hand, by the gravity, the weightiness of bodies and so of the real distances of a *whole* world and, on the other, by the absence of weight, of gravity, of the signals of a kind of visual and tactile high definition appropriate to the exotic arena of electromagnetic fields.

The life-size nature of *physical distances* having thus come under the law of the *microphysical power* of waves transmitting hearing and sight and soon touch (touch at a distance), how can we ignore the risk mankind runs of losing our own world? How can we but fear now a profound sense of being shut up in an environment deprived of both horizon and *optical density*?

When someone quoted to Edgar Degas Henri-Frédéric Amiel's romantic phrase, 'A landscape is a state of mind', the French painter retorted, '*No, it's not. It's a state of eye!*'

Today, when we are all so worried about the ecological balance of a human environment seriously threatened by industrial waste, would it not be appropriate to add to the concerns of *green ecology* those of a *grey ecology* that would focus on the postindustrial degradation of the depth of field of the terrestrial landscape?

★

The space probe Pioneer 10, launched on 2 March 1972, was the first man-made object to leave the solar system. But it was also, and perhaps first and foremost, *a sort of measuring rod of different cosmic magnitudes*. Located somewhere at *eight billion kilometres from Earth*, the American rocket each day sends signals that take *seven and a half hours* to reach the NASA antennae. With the telescope and the whole set of instruments aboard the probe remaining operational, the 'real time' of the messages transmitted by Pioneer is thus practically the same as the time difference between Tokyo and Paris.

A veritable electronic scanner of the scale of the universe, the space probe informs us continuously, with a slight delay in feedback, of the gradual constriction of the earth's reaches. Indeed, as Gustave Flaubert wrote, 'The better telescopes become, the more stars there will be.' But Flaubert forgot to mention the fallout from this sudden optical expansion: *the more perception of the otherworld develops, the less there will be of the world, of a whole earth!*

The more advanced our means of knowing what lies beyond the horizon become, the more the earth's expanses and the 'duration' of the world of tangible experience will diminish and be reduced to nothing, to less than nothing. This is what we might call *the wrong of the telescope.*

Note in passing that while small-scale geometric optics was once demonstrated by Galileo, large-scale optoelectronics, in once again showing mankind that *the earth turns*, sets itself the task of demonstrating that *the universe is expanding*. Two different *times*, two eras of perception and two radically different *motions*.

But let us return to our space probe, designed to observe the stars in the solar system at close range, in particular Jupiter. Propelled by that planet's gravitational force, the American rocket inexorably pursues its course towards infinity, at a speed of 46,000 kilometres per hour. But what *hour* and what *kilometre* are we talking about, since the probe has been moving away from all geographical landmarks for twenty-three years?

On its own, the automatic probe is in fact nowhere, so much so that the people responsible for its launch, today retired, such as B.J. O'Brien, can say: 'It's impressive, *it's even mind-boggling!*' In spite of the rational, scientific side of the law of *universal expansion*, established nearly sixty years ago by Edwin Hubble and company, no one can really take in the effects of such movement on ordinary perception, on immediate experience, while a huge phenomenon of attraction, of suction, is today soaking up the reality effect of terrestrial appearances.

Preoccupied as we are by the hole in the famous 'ozone layer', none of us has yet noticed this gradual dematerialization of the earth's horizon, this other 'hole' produced by the impending primacy of the **real-time perspective** of physical optics over that of the real space of the geometric optics of the Quattrocentro. The **big picture**, though, is a perfectly logical outcome of the famous **big bang** of contemporary astrophysics.

We might even legitimately now wonder whether Edwin Hubble, one of the founding fathers of *the principle of cosmic expansion* (thanks, notably, to the prowess of the Mount Wilson telescope), was not in 1929 the first victim of the optical illusion announced by Flaubert as, indeed, Albert Einstein seemed to suspect at the time. As for recent **big bang** apostles, they could also easily be 'victims of the set' of an astronomical light-emitting capacity enhanced by the signal transmission speed of telescopes and radio telescopes.

Magnification, optical diminution, Doppler effect of the redshifts observed in the spectrum of the galaxies: so many other names for the acceleration and deceleration (recessional velocity) of appearances, in which **dromoscopy** – the light of speed – *literally sheds light on perceptible reality*, a reality whose **stereoscopic relief** is already causing a number of perceptual disorders which we shall apparently have to face up to in the end, since the very notion of 'physical proximity' is in danger of finding itself radically changed. The **large-scale optics** that allows us to test the most vast astrophysical remoteness thus contributes, conversely, to the invalidation of the closest physical proximity.

We might observe, in confirmation of what I am saying, that twenty-three years ago, before the launch of the Pioneer space probe, the scientists decided it was a good idea to stick an identification tag on the rocket. On top of a representation of the solar system with planet Earth and the outlines of a man and a woman, the Americans added a hydrogen atom to give extraterrestrials some idea of our size, *the distance between the nucleus and its single electron defining the unit of measure*. Even though the probe about to be launched was designed to test the unimaginable enormity of cosmic expansion, its designers thereby reinstated the notion of 'minimum distance' in its role of evaluating that **life-size** that really is our original home.

Whether we like it or not, for each and every one of us there is now a split in the representation of the World and so in its *reality*. A split between activity and interactivity, presence and telepresence, existence and tele-existence.

Faced with the *stereoscopic* nature of a reality divided between optics and optoelectronics, acoustics and electroacoustics, touch and tele-tactility, we have been given notice to quit our customary ways of seeing and thinking, in order to apprehend a new kind of 'relief' that even goes as far as undermining the practical usefulness of the notion of *horizon* and, with it, the 'perspective' that previously allowed us to recognize ourselves *here and now*. All this has come about because the once unique source of 'light', and so of 'reality', of bygone days has itself been split in two: the (direct) shade of the sun's rays or of the electric lamp is now complemented by (indirect) 'shadow areas' of the lack of emission of electronic signals, *telesurveillance* suddenly springing up and supplanting the illumination of things, the ordinary observer's seeing *with his own eyes*.

As the first generation in history to witness the conquest of space but also, more importantly, the conquest of a speed enabling us to conquer the real time of instantaneity, we are now also witnessing the unveiling of a final form of energy, **kinematic energy**, 'image' energy or, if you prefer, 'information' energy, coming on top of potential and kinetic energies.

This third form of energy allows not only the **geometrization** of our vision of the world, along the lines of that of the Italian Renaissance perspectivists, but also its **digitization**, with the craft of appearances, elaborated by the proponents of the 'passive' optics of the space of matter, bowing out before the industry of the 'active' (optoelectronic) optics of the time of light.

In fact, when the relativists of Einstein's era replace the concept of physical 'distance' with the concept of an instantaneous microphysical transmitting and receiving 'power', thereby wiping out in one fell swoop the former primacy of the perspectivist conception of Galileo's era – and even adding a third interval of the 'light' type to the classic intervals of 'space' and 'time' – they produce a mutation in the reality principle whereby the *automatic* nature of representations means perception is standardized. This is made possible by the use of the synthetic energy of electronic imagery, and it occurs just as much in the area of 'analogue' representations as in 'digital' ones.

Note once again that, beyond the confines of proximity as we know it, prospective **telepresence** – and shared **tele-existence** with it – not only eliminate the 'line' of the visible horizon in favour of the linelessness of a deep and imaginary horizon. They also once again undermine the very notion of **relief**, with touch and **tactile telepresence at a distance** now seriously muddying not only the distinction between the 'real' and the 'virtual', as Cybersurfers currently define it, but also the very reality of the *near* and the *far*, thus casting doubt on our presence *here and now* and so dismantling the necessary conditions for sensory experience.

PART 2

THE LAW OF PROXIMITY

'Everything is ruled by lightning.'
Heraclitus

'See this mosquito? It's an incredible device with its tiny captors that can detect blood-carrying vessels. It makes an incision in the skin with a microscopic saw and sucks the blood with remarkable precision. If we were to build a machine of this kind, we could take blood and analyse it without you even feeling the sting. *Soon we will make microrobots that will take off on a mission to explore the human organism.*' So says the Vice President of Toyota Motor Corps's research laboratory.

And that is a promise: in the near future, the human body will become the training ground for micromachines that will travel through it in all directions and do so, they say, without causing any pain. So here then are the latest prostheses, the new automatons: these **animates** that will colonize our organism, just as we ourselves have colonized and controlled the expanse of the earth's body.

Today, when 99 per cent of all microelectronic machines produced are captors or sensors, and when motor vehicles (smart cars) are already equipped with over fifty microprocessor scanners of all kinds to control pressure, vibration or shock, *smart pills* are being concocted for the human organism that are capable of transmitting information long-distance concerning nerve function or blood flow; and later on we will have microrobots capable of circulating in our arteries to treat diseased tissue.

'Industry has already come up with the necessary microprocessors and sensors; all we have to do now is add the arms and legs,' explains Professor Fujita of Tokyo University.

Having reached this stage in the development of the postindustrial machine, the question of the *miniaturization* of components becomes crucial in analysing the *topology of technology*. In fact, while the history of technology has accustomed us to weighing up the growing importance of industrial machinery both in terms of volume and geography, with the proliferation of railways, cables, high tension lines or networks of highways, we are suddenly now seeing the reverse process: little by little, *technological reductionism* is spreading to all branches of communications and telecommunications. The law of mechanical proximity that once allowed us to carve up and develop the human environment, the 'exogenous' environment of the species, is giving way to a law of electromagnetic proximity about which we really know nothing and understand even less. And soon, as more or less passive witnesses, we shall see the imminent invasion of our bodies, the control of an 'endogenous' environment, that of our entrails and viscera, thanks to the interactive feats of a biotechnological miniaturization that will finish off the job of those flourishing large-scale mass communications tools that already govern our society.

So the genealogy of technology will have taken us slowly from control of the *geophysical* environment, thanks to the development of the hydraulic networks and engineering involved in the cadastral organization of the world, to control of the *physical* environment, with mechanics and the physical chemistry of the energies fuelling the vectors of transport and communication, before ending today in control of the *microphysical* environment – not only of the climate, but of human physiology, the traditional pharmacopoeia making way for the interactive capabilities of transmission tools that human beings may soon ingest, indeed digest.

We are effectively seeing the beginnings of a third revolution:

following the transport revolution of the nineteenth century, which saw the flourishing of the railway system, followed by the automobile and aviation, we have, in the twentieth century, seen a second revolution, the transmission revolution, as a result of the implementation of the properties of instantaneous propagation of electromagnetic radiation in the form of radio and video. Behind closed laboratory doors, the *transplantation revolution* is now secretly gearing up, not only with the grafting of livers, kidneys, hearts and lungs, but with the implantation of new kinds of *stimulators*, much more effective than the pacemaker, and the imminent grafting of micromotors capable of overcoming the defective functioning of this or that natural organ and so improving on the vital performance of this or that physiological system belonging to a person in perfect health – thanks to scanners that can be accessed instantly at a distance.

Here, once again, the precise question of the topology of technologies is posed. I mean that mutation in the celebrated 'law of proximity' or, if you prefer, the law of least effort or least action. To reduce, to eliminate the range of action to the point of introducing a machine, a tool of instantaneous communication, into the human body's very guts poses awesome questions about the new technological environment, the postindustrial 'technosphere'.

Indeed, *acting at a distance* renders problematic the very nature of the interval that makes up this distance. *An interval of the space type* (negative sign) for the geometric development and control of the geophysical environment. *An interval of the time type* (positive sign) for control of the physical environment and the invention of communication tools. And, lastly, *an interval of the light type* (neutral sign), the third and ultimate interval (interface), for instantaneous control of the microphysical environment thanks to the new tools of telecommunications.

Before returning to the need to redefine the law of proximity because of the very instantaneity of interactive teletechnologies, we might observe that if control of prior geophysical and physical environments was rigorously contemporaneous with the absolute nature of space and time in Newton's era, control of the microphysical environment is contemporaneous with the absolute nature of the speed of light in Einstein's.

Today, if teletechnology's remote action winds up transplanting information sources into the very heart of the living being, this is because the law of 'electromagnetic' proximity has once and for all outstripped the law of 'mechanical' proximity, teleaction in future prevailing over immediate action.

Let us turn now to the evolution of transport and communication tools in their relation to the status of the body of the passer-by, the passenger, in anticipation of the future 'interactive' implant recipient.

To begin with, by breeding and domesticating a *draught* animal that could pull a harness or carry a useful load, man aligned himself with the mule, the ox or the horse, which he then guided, steered and finally rode, after managing to hop up on a chariot following the invention of the wheel.

He was also to hit on the idea of yoking the animal vehicle, his steed; he mounts the horse which then becomes a 'mount' and, shortly afterwards, an animal with *a saddle*, and not just a simple beast of burden any more.

This gave rise to the conquest of immense territories and to gradual control of humanity's geographic environment.

Finally, after the sailing ship, responsible for conquest of the seas and oceans, he was to invent the *motor* vehicle, a vehicle no longer 'metabolic' but technical – the locomotive with its carriages, the car, the plane – which he would move into permanently, so that 'inside driving', driving under cover, from that moment won out over the old mount.

With the revolution in broadcasting hot on the heels of the transport revolution, telecommunication equipment was to adapt to the body of the individual which was then fitted out with communications prostheses: the mobile phone, walkman, portable computer or TV, electrodes, to say nothing of the DataGlove or DataSuit, in anticipation of the future transplantation revolution and the ingurgitation of micromachines, *the technological fuelling of the living body* in which the ingredients or substances ingested will not just be foodstuffs produced by the physical chemistry of nutrients known as 'restoratives', but will include substances produced by microprocessors, by more or less biodegradable 'stimulant' implants, microbe-machines, cellular automata allegedly able to improve certain of our faculties.

So, in the same way as the new materials are enriched from within their outer layers by sundry networks, optical fibres, fibre-optic cables or integrated circuit microprocessors made of substances either cast or moulded, woven or thermoformed, the intimate space of the innards of the human body is preparing to receive its complement of 'intra-organic' micromachinery. And this micromachinery will be *capable of acting*, not only in the manner of Doctor Delgado's famous electrodes but, this time, along remote control lines, with enough zapping of vital functions – as with alcohol or narcotics – to 'wake the dead'. A biotechnical, and not merely biochemical, straitjacket, whereby the psychophysiology of an individual's behaviour would be permanently relayed to instantaneous information capabilities, his/her body wired with electronic pathways that would extend the nervous system. Things have already gone so far that certain researchers are proposing to build completely new equipment, *molecule by molecule*, nanomachines being merely, in their view, the first stage in an evolution that will in future take them from simple cells to more complex organisms.

This 'endogenous' mechanization will then sweep aside the 'exogenous' mechanization that allows us to control humanity's geophysical environment.

But let's get back to this latest law of proximity and its relationship to the principle of least action. If the recent evolution of post-industrial machinery is anything to go by: **less is more**. Not only in terms of the volume or the physical cumbersomeness of the object, but equally in terms of the material and the internal construction of the microscopic motor. The burning question is: *if less is more, to what extent?* To the point where it reaches the virtual, where it becomes this *image*, this virtual reality that is ultimately more decisive than the *thing* which it is merely the image of?

Since the current miniaturization entails a corollary dematerialization of the appliance, we need to ask ourselves if there is a limit – quantum or otherwise – to the process of reduction and virtualization of the contemporary technological object.

Present or, more precisely, 'telepresent' man no longer actually inhabits the energy of any machinery whatsoever. *It is energy that instantaneously inhabits and governs him*, whether he likes it or not. A radical reversal of the principle of least action that had till now shaped social history. Besides, it is clear what the project of the coming transplant revolution is. It is *to miniaturize the world*, having reduced and miniaturized its components, the technological objects the world has contained ever since industry first took off.

So, what about the future of architecture, of that domestic space where daily proximity collected, as much in the interval of residential rooms as in the terracing of the apartment block.

If the possibility of acting instantaneously *without having to move about physically* to open the blinds, switch on the light or adjust the heating has partly removed the practical value of space and time intervals to the sole benefit of the *speed interval* of remote control (thanks to the feats of the **live** transmission revolution), what will happen when this capacity for action or, rather, for instantaneous interaction, with the biotechnological transplant revolution, migrates from the thickness of the walls or floors of the wired apartment and settles not on, but inside, the body of the inhabitants, introducing itself, lodging itself inside their bodies, in the closed circuits of their vital systems?

Bear in mind once again the peculiar nature of this *law of least action*: where there is a choice between a lift or an escalator and a simple staircase to reach upper floors, no one takes the stairs. Similarly, where a metro corridor is too long and there is a moving walkway (a travolator) at the users' disposal, no one traipses along the corridor. The same goes for telecommunications: it is better to send an electric impulse than to carry a sheet of paper, but carrying a letter, sending mail, is better than sending a messenger.[1] This rule extends as far as the notions, crucial in architecture, of **inside** and **outside**, which are gradually losing their importance. With the immateriality of electromagnetic radiation, even the difference between **high** and **low** is being eroded, despite the fact that this difference is a major part of putting buildings up!

In a recent interview, the architect Kazuo Shinohara claimed: 'The future city is the pleasure of the interval.'[2]

But what 'interval' are we talking about here, with the decline in time distances and so in the requirements of physical movement?

With the supremacy of the *interval of absolute speed* (third interval of the neutral-sign light type) of electronic waves that enable interactivity to occur and so the sudden relativization of the intervals of space (negative sign) and time (positive sign), all the conceptual bases of architectonics are literally collapsing, right up to that natural lighting provided by the sun which we can now conduct, via sensors and optical fibres, from the roof-garden of the apartment block into the inside of the apartment, *the fibrous space of the cable taking over from the opening of windows in the facade of the home.*

So, what can we say about the effect of the impending introduction of such teletechnologies, such transplant procedures into man's inner body as well as over the arrangement of his domestic environment? Already, with the transport revolution of the nineteenth century, movement from one place to another had obviously undergone a mutation, since 'departure' and 'arrival' at a destination were peculiarly privileged to the detriment of the 'journey' properly so called. Note in this connection the passivity, the somnolence of bullet train passengers and the screening of films on long-haul planes. With the instantaneous transmission revolution, it is now 'departure' that gets wiped out and 'arrival' that gets promoted, *the generalized arrival of data*, from television to telecommuting, to the teleaction made possible by remote control of the domestic systems of the smart house.

Wired to control the environment without actually moving a limb, *a teleoperator of their own surroundings*, deprived of those exotic prostheses with which the neighbourhood of the city was once rigged out, the inhabitant of the teletopical metacity can no longer clearly distinguish *here* from *elsewhere*, private from public. The insecurity of their *territorial hold* extends from the space of their own world to the space of their own body. Once this happens, adoption of a sedentary life tends to become final, absolute, since the functions traditionally distributed within the real space of the town are now exclusively taken over by the real time of the wiring of the human body.

The key notions of (radio, video, digital) signal input and output have overtaken those usually associated with the movement of people or objects traditionally distributed throughout the extension of space.

The short-circuiting of intention and the will to act then replaces acting by means of gestures and body movements.

Contrary to traditional mechanical proximity, the new electromagnetic proximity is not so much spatial as temporal. The real time of immediacy (live coverage) dominates the real space of the building, requiring the builder completely to overhaul his working notions and necessitating a perspective in which time, interactivity's duration (or more precisely, its lack of duration) prevails over the geometric space of the Quattrocento.

The old conception of architecture, based on the 'absolute' nature of the intervals of space and time of volumetric analysis, ceases to be relevant. After Newton, the relativization of these notions opens on to the absolutism of the speed of light and the emergence of a last type of interval of *neutral sign* that will in turn demand a new perspective, *the accelerated perspective of real time*, as well as the invention of new theories of architecture and urbanism.[3]

And so, the law of electromagnetic proximity creates compelling necessities that not only concern ethics or the politics of energy, but also aesthetics and our vision of the world.

The sudden bewildering Babel clamour of the world-city, the untimely mix of the *global* and the *local*, of which the Gulf War was an early-warning sign, are ringing in the next revolution: the biotechnological transplant revolution, the rigging out of our animal bodies with the same road maintenance networks and highways that have until now rigged out the territorial body of urban society.

The last 'territory', human physiology thus becomes the privileged site of experimentation for the micromachines of communications: drugs, anabolic steroids and dope appearing as clinical symptoms of this coming sensory permutation.

I do not know if, as Shinohara goes on to claim, *the city of the future will express the beauty of confusion*. I am, on the other hand, quite convinced that it will in the near future illustrate the tragedy of the fusion of the 'biological' and the 'technological'.

GREY ECOLOGY

'The inert man gets in his own way.'
Seneca

Alongside the pollution of the **substances** that make up our environment, which ecologists are always harping about, surely we should also be able to detect the sudden pollution of **distances** and lengths of time that is degrading the expanse of our habitat.

Being eternally preoccupied by the pollution of **nature**, are we not deliberately overlooking this pollution of **life-size** that reduces to nothing earth's scale and size?

While citizenship and civility depend not only on 'blood' and 'soil', as we keep being told, but also, and perhaps especially, on the nature and proximity of human groups, would it not be more appropriate to come up with a different kind of ecology? A discipline less concerned with **nature** than with the effects of the artificial environment of the town on the degradation of the physical proximity of beings, of different communities. Proximity of the immediate neighbourhood of different parts of town; 'mechanical' proximity of the lift, the train or the car and lastly, most recently, electromagnetic proximity of instantaneous telecommunications.

So many connections broken: from the soil, the neighbourhood unit, one's fellow human beings, be they relatives, friends, or next-door neighbours. The **media-staged** gap is no longer just a matter of the too great distance between the urban centre and its suburbs or periphery; it also involves televisual intercommunication, fax, home shopping and sex hotlines.

As 'citizens of the world' and inhabitants of nature, we too often forget that we also inhabit physical dimensions, the scale of space and the lengths of time of the *life-size*. The obvious degradation of the elements, chemical or other, that make up the substances comprising our natural surroundings has joined forces with the unperceived pollution of the distances that organize our relationships with others, and also with the world of sense experience. Whence the urgency of backing up the ecology of nature with an ecology of the contrivances of transport and transmission technologies that literally *exploit* the size of the geophysical environment and damage its scope.

'Speed destroys colour: when a gyroscope is spinning fast everything goes grey,' wrote Paul Morand in 1937, in the middle of the new paid holidays. Today, when the extreme proximity of telecommunications is putting paid to the extreme speed limit of supersonic communication tools, would it not be appropriate to set up a **grey** ecology alongside the **green**? An ecology of those 'archipelagos of cities', intelligent and interconnected, that will soon reshape Europe and the world.

It is in this context of a space-time turned on its head by the teletechnologies of action at a distance that we can effectively speak of an **urban ecology**. An ecology that would be concerned not only with the air and noise pollution of the big cities but, first and foremost, the sudden eruption of the 'world-city', totally dependent on telecommunications, that is being put in place at the end of the millennium.

Long-haul tourism, celebrated by Paul Morand in his day, is now rounded off by a sort of 'on-the-spot tourism' based on cocooning and interactivity.

'You have turned a world into a town,' the Gallo-Roman Namatianus chided Caesar. This imperial project has recently become an everyday reality, a fact we can no longer ignore, either economically or, more especially, culturally. Hence the end of the town–country opposition which we are seeing in Europe, following the Third World's lead, with the depopulation of a rural space now delivered up to idleness, full of land left lying fallow – the intellectual 'shrinking' that such an urban supremacy supposes requiring, it would seem, another 'intelligence' of the artificial and not merely another policy on nature.

At the precise moment when the necessary direct transparence of the 'optical' layer of the terrestrial atmosphere is being overlaid with the indirect transparence of the 'optoelectronic' (and electroacoustic) layer of the empire of *real-time* telecommunications, we cannot long go on ignoring the damage done by progress in an area ecologists have completely overlooked: the area of *relativity*, that is, of a new relationship to the places and time distances created by the broadcasting revolution, with the recent implementation of the absolute speed of electromagnetic radiation. Even if the transport revolution, which only implemented the relative speeds of the train, the plane or the automobile, seems to hold no interest for disciples of the 'environmental sciences', except for the disastrous effects its associated infrastructures (highways, high-speed railways and airports) may have on the landscape.

Oriental wisdom has it that *time is useful when it is not used*. Surely we can say the same of space, the unused life-size of the expanse of a world unknown and often ignored.

Today, faced with the decline in geography, now converted into an abstract *science of space*, and the disappearance of exoticism with the boom in tourism and mass communication equipment, surely we should be asking ourselves in all urgency about the meaning and cultural importance of geophysical dimensions.

In the sixteenth century, Jérôme Cardan noted in his autobiography:

'I was born into a century in which the whole earth had been discovered, whereas the Ancients scarcely knew a third of it.'[1]

What can we say at the end of this twentieth century which saw the first moon landing, except that we have exhausted the time of the finite world, standardized the earth's expanse?

Whether we like it or not, races are always *eliminative*, not only for the competitors engaged in the competition, but also for the environment underlying their efforts. Whence the invention of an artificial arena, of a 'stage' on which to practise the exploit of extreme speed: stadium, hippodrome or autodrome. Such an instrumentalization of space signalling a tailoring, not only of the body of the athlete, trained to exceed his own limits, or the bodies of the racehorses in our stables, but also of the **geometry** of the environment supporting such motor performances: *the closed-circuit connection* of all those vast sporting amenities heralding the closed-loop connection, the final looping and locking up of a world that has become *orbital*, not only in terms of circumterrestrial satellites on the beat, but of the entire array of telecommunications tools as well.

And so, after the expropriated land of railways and of a system of highways that has now become continental, one last form of pollution is becoming a concrete reality: the pollution of the geographical expanse by supersonic transport and the new telecommunications tools. With the damage that this now presupposes to the sense of reality we each possess, as the world becomes meaningless now it is no longer so much **whole** as **reduced** by technologies that have acquired, in the course of the twentieth century, the absolute speed of electromagnetic waves – on top of the speed required to 'get off the rock': 'orbital velocity' at 28,000 kilometres per hour.

Whence the urgent political necessity of scrapping the *law of least effort* that has always been behind our technology boom, a law utterly vital to us and one based, like the law of the astronomical movement of the planets, on *gravity*, that force of universal attraction that at once lends weight, meaning and direction to the objects that make up the human environment.

If the 'accident' helps in understanding the 'substance', the accident of falling bodies reveals to all and sundry the **quality** of our environment, its specific weightiness.

Since it is *use* that defines terrestrial space, the environment, we cannot cover any expanse or therefore any (geophysical) 'quantity' except through the effort of more or less lasting (physical) motion, through the fatigue of a journey where the only void that exists exists by nature of the action undertaken in order to cross it.

So, the 'ecological' question of the **nature** of our habitat cannot be resolved unless we also try to find the connection linking 'space' and 'effort', the duration and extent of a physical fatigue that gives the world of tangible experience its measure, its 'life-size' quality. The lack of effort involved in teletechnologies for hearing, seeing or acting at a distance obliterates all direction, the vastness of the earth's horizon. It remains to us now to discover the 'new world': not the world of the far-flung antipodes that we discovered five centuries ago, but a world where proximity has no future, where the technologies of *real time* will soon prevail over those that once shaped the *real space* of the planet.

If being *present* really does mean being *close*, physically speaking, the *microphysical* proximity of interactive telecommunication will surely soon see us staying away in droves, not being there any more for anyone, locked up, as we shall be, in a *geophysical* environment reduced to less than nothing.

'The world has shrunk, shrunk unbelievably; we no longer travel, we get around.'[2]

This lone sailor's lament once again sets the question of limits, the limits of a world in the grip of doubt, but also of disorientation, in which the markers of position and location are disappearing one by one in the face of progress. Not progress in the acceleration of historical knowledge any more but, this time, in the acceleration of geographical knowledge, the very notions of scale and physical dimension gradually losing their meaning in the face of the infinite fragmentation of point of view.

At the turn of the century, Karl Kraus quipped: '*An adjustible horizon cannot be tight.*'[3]

Now let's hear it from an expert on the horizon of television: '*Since the space of the screen is pretty small, the programme can't be too long.*'

That about sums it up. Where the display space is reduced, the pace has to pick up so that what is lacking in extension can be put back in duration! The perspective of the (real) life-size space of a world still full, still whole, is now of necessity saddled with a relativistic perspective of time: that real time of an instantaneity that makes up for the definitive loss of geophysical distances.

It is interesting to note as well that, in these times of virtual navigation and periscopic immersion in the cybernetic world, it should once again be mariners who are the first to express the sense of lost reality. In the journal he kept of crossing the Pacific by raft, Gérard d'Aboville writes: 'To reach my goal, I had to create a mental universe *in which the distance travelled reigned supreme*. A fragile universe, since now I'm no longer making headway, the temptation to give up looms.'[4]

To give up locomotive force, in other words, to die.

A parable of the history of universal navigation, of the headway made in knowledge of the world's limits, whereby *distance* has followed navigators around in the same way as the *substance* of the seas, and this up to the untimely elimination of all maritime or continental expanses, with the acquisition of the supreme speed of waves – electromagnetic ones this time.

So, entrapment within the circumterrestrial space of a geophysical reality made up of the sound and the fury of the oceans will shortly be succeeded by imprisonment in the 'real time' of a microphysical (virtual) reality, the result of a **transhorizon** perspective, the veritable 'time barrier' of this no-delay time of the speed of light that has suddenly put the finishing touches to the effects of breaking the barriers of sound and heat: a feat which has enabled man to free himself from earth's gravitation and to land on the shores of the night star.

Once, each generation of human beings had to try and find out how *deep* the wide world was for themselves, to free themselves from their familiar neighbourhood and discover distant horizons. Travel is the best education, they used to say.

In the near future, each generation will inherit an *optical layer* of reality thinned out by the effect of a perspective both fundamentally 'temporal' and 'atemporal' *at the same time*. And this will enable them – at birth, or as good as – to perceive the **end of the world**, the narrowness of a habitat instantaneously accessible no matter what the geographical distance.

This is a pollution no longer atmospheric or hydrospheric but **dromospheric** that will soon see the semblance bowing out, the geophysical reality of this 'territorial body' without which neither the 'social body' nor the 'animal body' could exist, since being means *being situated – in situ* – here and now, *hic et nunc*.

'What doth it profit a man if he gain the whole world, but lose his only soul', his *anima*, that which moves him and allows him to be both animated and loving, allows him to draw towards himself not only the other, *otherness*, but the environment, *proximity*, by moving from place to place.

An Armenian proverb puts it well: 'If my heart is narrow, what is the good of the world being so wide?'

True distances, the true measure of the earth, lie in my heart. For animals, distance is only ever a time distance. Man, along with seagulls and spiders, carries the expanse of the environment around with him, in motion, in animation. Forty thousand kilometres around the Earth is nothing. The measurements of geography exist only for geographers and cartographers who want to determine the distance from one point to another. For the living being, this metric gauge will never equal the size of the world.

For whoever exists distance is nothing more than knowledge, memory and analogy. With the different technologies of (supersonic) transport and (hypersonic) transmission, we find ourselves in the position of someone who has been warned by the weather report that it will rain the next day: that person's today, their lovely day is ruined, *already ruined*, and they have quickly to make hay. As in the example of the small screen necessitating the acceleration of televised sequences, here it is the urgency of the present that makes itself felt.

But the tragic thing in this temporal perspective is that what is thereby polluted, fundamentally damaged, is no longer just the immediate future, the sense of what the weather will be like, but the space that is *already there*, the sense that the environment is missing: in a word, *the death of geography*.

'Travel is a kind of doorway through which you leave reality as though you were entering an unexplored reality that seems like a dream,' wrote Guy de Maupassant.

With the state of emergency in time distances, that dream fades, soon to be replaced by the **telex** or by immersion in virtual reality. Everything is *déjà vu* or at least *déjà exploré*: been there, done that. The impossibility of seeing is followed by the impossibility of not seeing, of not foreseeing.

General travel has already replaced the special trip: the voyage of the navigator or the trek of the lone explorer. The tourism of the televiewer or telecommuter is the eternal return of a feedback, a 'crusade' that has reached its destination.

After the window, long since replaced by the telesurveillance screen, it is now the gate, *the gateway*, that comes into its own on the threshold of the space of virtual navigation. After the circle of the horizon and the surface of the transhorizon screen, it is now the *volume* of cyberspace that holds sway. Telematic information has thus become the third dimension, the **relief**, of tangible reality, but of a 'reality' that escapes the real space of ordinary geography only to re-emerge in the real time of the transmission-reception of interactive signals.

The *vanishing-point* of the original perspective (geometric optics) of real space of the Quattrocento, is superseded by the *vanishing of all points* (pixels, data bits) in the second perspective (physical optics) of real time of the Novocento.

Here information not only becomes the third dimension of matter, along with mass and energy, as the pioneers of 'computer science' once argued. It becomes the **final relief** of reality, a reality as calculable as the surface of the painting once was for the original perspectivists, a *virtual reality* that offers every one of us the considerable advantage of being both more 'real' than imagination and more easily controlled than concrete reality.

But what 'relief' are we talking about here, when the World has shrunk to such an extent that claustrophobia has suddenly become a major danger for humanity? When the *time depth* of instantaneity once and for all elbows aside the *depth of field* of humanity's space, what 'optical layer' is there left to speak of?

Fatally confusing the visible horizon against which all 'scenes' stand out and the deep horizon of the imaginary, this final *relief* is indeed not unlike that of a *phantom limb*, a virtual presence perceived as an integral part of the mutilated body.

Note that in such cases, the presence of a prosthesis further accentuates the maimed person's perception of a limb that has in fact gone.

Has Mother Earth become humanity's phantom limb?

Doesn't the development of telecommunications prosthetics accentuate the 'ghostly dimension' of a vision of the world from now on computer-enhanced?

This is what Franz Kafka had to say, in a letter written to Milena in 1922: 'Humanity senses this and fights against it and in order to eliminate as far as possible the ghostly element between people and to create a natural communication, the peace of souls, it has invented the railway, the motor car, the aeroplane. But it's no longer any good, these are evidently inventions being made at the moment of crashing. *The opposing side is so much calmer and stronger,* after the postal service it has invented the telegraph, the telephone, the radiograph. *The ghosts won't starve, but we will perish.*'[5]

What more is there to say, except that we have since invented television and the reality of a virtual space that will allow us to interact long-distance and no matter what the distance from our neighbour? Will we, in the near future, have to *'love our non-neighbour as we love ourselves'*?

If this were so, the question of 'up to what point' would no longer even arise, since the lack of any limit apart from the cosmological constant of the speed of reality waves would quickly induce us to practise long-distance love. Not the 'courtly love' of the Middle Ages any more, but the 'virtual love' permitted by the sensory feats of **cybersex**, with demographic consequences for humanity that go without saying thanks to the invention of such a **universal condom**!

'Whatever moves between heaven and Earth can only be explained in terms of heaven and Earth,' wrote Ernst Jünger, paraphrasing the philosophers of Antiquity on the sublunar world. By way of conclusion, we might point out that our 'grey ecology' is in the end not far removed from that 'ontology' of the same colour or, rather, the same absence of colour: the old speculation about *being in itself.* But this particular *in itself* concerns the immediate conjunction of *being here and now,* being located *in this world.* This world of earth's gravitation that gives the world both its weight and its measure. But also, conversely, *the will to escape weightiness through flight*, the narrow escape of a fall upwards, beyond the geophysical limits that are humanity's lot. An overcoming of all 'resistance to forward motion' that makes man like an angel, the being like a bird, since we all know from experience that: '*What does not come down, flies*.'[6]

But there remains an imprescriptible limit to this historic movement of emancipation, and that is the limit of its **acceleration**.

Despite the recent acquisition of what astrophysicists call **escape velocity**, the acceleration that has enabled man to be freed from his habitat is not the 'liberation' it was made out to be. For real liberation is only possible, *as effective liberation from all movement of displacement*, through implementation of the constant of the speed of light in a vacuum. This is a **real-time barrier** at which, having successfully broken the barriers of sound and heat, humanity finally attains the behavioural inertia that causes us to lose our angelic attributes, to shed our 'wings', in a fall from – a forfeiting of – grace into a corpse-like fixedness which is, admittedly, relative, but final as far as our relationship with the world of physical experience goes.

In conclusion, here is a tale that dates from this sudden 'end of the world': '*During my space flight, I had the strange impression time was being compressed*, as though speed had the effect of piling up moments spent inside the capsule on top of one another. All the time I had the feeling of being rushed from one event to the next as they popped up, like ducks in a shooting gallery,' wrote Scott Carpenter in his journal of a voyage around the globe effected at a speed of 27,000 kilometres per hour, thus describing a new form of zapping, no longer televisual, but visual.[7]

CONTINENTAL DRIFT

'Nothing is as vast as empty things.'
Francis Bacon

In the realm of territorial development, 'time' now counts more than 'space'. But it is no longer a matter of some chronological *local time*, as it once was, but of universal *world time*, opposed not only to the local space of a region's organization of land, but to the world space of a planet on the way to becoming homogeneous.

From the urbanization of the real space of national geography to the urbanization of the real time of international telecommunications, the 'world space' of geopolitics is gradually yielding its strategic primacy to the 'world time' of a chronostrategic proximity without any delay and without any antipodes.

But the *metropolitics* that results from this sudden uniqueness of the world time of instantaneous telecommunications also implies the emergence of a very new type of accident: until now, with the supremacy of local space-time, each of us was still exposed only to a *specific accident*, one precisely located; with the emergence of world time, however, we will all be exposed (or, more precisely, over-exposed) to the *general accident*, the delocalization of action and reaction (interaction) necessarily implying *the delocalization of all accidents*.

Finally, with the revolution in the electromagnetic transmission of images, of sound and information, you could say that *the traffic accident finally has a future* since, above and beyond the classic accidents of rail, air, sea or road, we will soon see the emergence of *the accident to end all accidents*, in other words, *the traffic of the generalized accident* which will then largely outdo the *limited* traffic accident of the transport revolution.[1]

To a certain extent, the Chernobyl nuclear catastrophe already fore-shadowed the scale of the major accident of tomorrow. Indeed, while *radioactivity* was able to circulate with impunity from East to West, contaminating entire continents in passing, the electromagnetic transmission system of the *interactivity* of future information super-highways is part of the same phenomenon of global reach.

As we know, without instantaneity and ubiquity (attributes of the divine now applied to the human) of action and reaction, there would never have been such a major risk of accidentally triggering *the general accident* – in other words, the historic accident of the trans-fer of the supremacy of the *localized* time of the facts and gestures belonging to each of us here and now, to the *globalized* time of gen-eralized interaction between everyone in the same instant.

A phenomenon with no known precedent outside the realms of theology and astrophysics, it is part and parcel of the general spread of **information** as a theoretical notion to the detriment of those practical notions of **mass** and **energy** that made history.

Implicitly doing away with the 'historic' time of **politics** – more precisely, of geopolitics – and exclusively promoting the 'anti-historic' time of the **media**, the general spread of real-time information causes a radical divide beside which the industrial revo-lution will pale into insignificance.

In such conditions, how can we claim to forecast the future, when history and geography themselves will soon cease to be what they once were: the necessary foundations of all futurology?

How can we attempt to extrapolate some sort of 'statistical trend' when we are already living under the alarming pressure of an unprecedented temporal breakdown, in the throes of an imminent *social crash* whose early-warning bells are already going off here and there, with the effects of structural unemployment and of reversion of the family to the state?

The global metropolitics of the future electronic information highways in itself implies the coming of a society no longer divided so much into North and South, but into two distinct temporalities, two speeds: one *absolute*, the other *relative*. The gap between developed and underdeveloped countries being reinforced throughout the five continents and leading to an even more radical divide between those who will live under the empire of real time essential to their economic activities at the heart of the virtual community of the *world city*, and those, more destitute than ever, who will survive in the real space of *local towns*, that great planetary wasteland that will in future bring together the only too real community of those who no longer have a job or a place to live that are likely to promote harmonious and lasting socialization. Not long ago, Paul Valéry warned: 'The time of the finite world is beginning.' It is time we faced facts. Today, it is the reverse that is happening before our very eyes: *the world of finite time (global time) is beginning.*

Similarly, while modern philosophers claim that *the substance* is essential and *the accident* relative and contingent, the postmodernists say we are seeing a reversal of this, term for term, since it is the accident that becomes *absolute* and substance, any and every substance, *relative* and contingent.

Like some gigantic implosion, the circulation of the general accident of communication technologies is building up and spreading, forcing all substances to keep moving in order to interact globally, at the risk of being wiped out, being swallowed up completely. Like the internationalized industry or business forced to relocate its production facilities and then, due to the high level of mobility of competing goods, suddenly also to relocate its official headquarters, using the *just-in-time* inventory system (JIT: precision scheduling of supplies designed to minimize stockholding).

To illustrate the point, take the example of a manufacturer set up in France on the borders of the Maine and the Loire-Atlantique. In 1988, his firm was already feeling the pinch of the initial globalization of markets; the director therefore decided to relocate part of production to southern Europe: more specifically, to Portugal.[2] A year later in 1989, when wages in Portugal were rising by 15 per cent, the French industrialist then found more attractive conditions of remuneration in Morocco; he took the plunge and crossed the Straits of Gibraltar, lowering the prices of his goods to below those charged by the direct competition – sending all his national subcontractors to the wall in the process.

More than three hundred people worked for our small businessman in Morocco until that country's inevitable wage hike drove him to take an even greater plunge and shift to Asia in 1992, where he imported into France from Korea clothes produced by subcontractors in Bangladesh. Finally, in 1993, our industrialist discovered Vietnam, where the army uses troops as indentured labour and there are workshops or, rather, barracks, where the work is paid at no more than two francs an hour. But it is already too late. The central buying offices are in place, ruling out any real competition.

About as convincing as the fable in which the hare beats the tortoise, this little episode beautifully illustrates the evolution of the firm in the postindustrial age.

Indeed, since commercial logistics serving consumer interests dominate business strategy, at the workers' expense, the industrial concern ends up failing. The just-in-time worldwide market relocation, like any military operation that goes on for too long, leads to the exhaustion of the forces of the firm concerned. And also, for it is a law specific to communications, *to the defeat of the commercial facts*, since the gradual disintegration of *real* small or medium-sized firms sets up a chain reaction from firm to firm that extends as far as the multinational corporations themselves and, ultimately, as far as the most powerful *virtual monopolies*, the coming crash of postindustrial production modes no longer being in any doubt.

At the end of his life Maurice Merleau-Ponty wrote: 'When science has learned to recognize the value of what it initially rejected as subjective, this will gradually be reintroduced – though incorporated as a specific case in the relationships and objects that define the world as science sees it. *The world will then close in on itself, and, except for whatever in us thinks and does science, the impartial observer that lives inside us, we will have become a part or a moment in the Great Object.*'

Since globalization will have caused the planet to close in on itself like a ripe fruit, how can we envisage the *geopolitical* development of French territory at the heart of continental Europe in twenty years' time, when the (interactive) *metropolitics* of telecommunications will have extended the reign of real time and the totality of the distances of real space will have finally given out in the face of the lack of delay of proliferating interaction?

After the no man's land of the desertified countrysides, how can we imagine the future no man's time of a planet where the interval of continental local space will have ceded primacy to the interface of the world time of information highways?

Let us not forget that the 'law of least action' that has always compelled the technosciences to go one better, has seen three successive kinds of proximity making up geopolitical history, the first of these being *metabolic* proximity, the second, *mechanical* proximity (the transport revolution). *Electromagnetic* proximity, the third and last kind of proximity, stemming from the transmission revolution, has this peculiarity: it goes against the grain of the experience of the very real proximity of people, the political capability of bringing populations together in one spot, whether that be a country or an urban agglomeration. And, in so doing, it promotes the long-distance meeting of telepresent interlocutors, thanks to the artefact of a now virtual proximity that no longer requires the immediacy of the concrete presence of other people. A presence that was, however, the very cornerstone of the geopolitics of nations. What gains by this is a metropolitics of instantaneity, a product of telecommunication's urbanization of time, which then succeeds the urbanization of regional space.

So the **metropolization** that we should fear for the coming century involves not so much concentration of populations in this or that 'city network', as the hyperconcentration of the *world-city*, the city to end all cities, a virtual city of which every real city will ultimately be merely a suburb, a sort of **omnipolitan** periphery whose *centre will be nowhere and circumference everywhere*.[3] The society of tomorrow will splinter into two opposing camps: those who live to the beat of the real time of the global city, within the virtual community of the 'haves', and the 'have-nots' who survive in the margins of the real space of local cities, even more abandoned than those living today in the suburban wastelands of the Third World.

Faced with this sudden *split of the facts* between 'reality' and 'virtuality', in which the *far* wins out over the *near*, the traditional categories of liberalism and authoritarianism will soon undergo a considerable mutation, since the **citizen** will be forced to bow out before the **contemporary**, media representation winning out by a long way over the classic political representation of nations.[4]

Besides, since the citizen was not effectively any such thing, except within the law of the *concrete reality* of the city-state, or of colonial and then national assemblies, the forecast decline in the reality of local city communities and the proliferation of the global city's *discrete virtuality* results in the increasing unreality of the legitimate state's territorial foundation. This privileges **contemporaneity** unfairly over **citizenship** and so causes the metropolitical virtuality of the **live broadcast** to dominate the geopolitical reality of the **town**.

In these basically eccentric or, if you like, **omnipolitan** conditions, the various social and cultural realities that still constitute a nation's wealth will soon give way to a sort of 'political' **stereoreality** in which the interaction of exchanges will no longer look any different from the – automatic – interconnection of financial markets today. Practices not too far removed in the end from the cybernetic systems previously denounced by the likes of Norbert Wiener, who already feared the tyranny of information.

Let us take a look now at a few events that typify what we have just been examining. In January 1994, IBM announced its intention to abandon its corporate headquarters, situated close to New York. This sudden decision on the part of such an important firm *to move to nowhere* looks like a major symptom of the transformation that may soon endanger the workplace – and not only the manufacturing plant or the administrative office, but equally, the significance of the city centre. Several factors are already contributing to this post-industrial overhaul. On the one hand, as we know, globalization of the economy has made overall re-evaluation of company strategy imperative to achieve corporate downsizing, with restructuring and pruning of labour costs. On the other hand, and simultaneously, the evolution of communication technologies has made it possible to get the job done no matter where you are.

Tomorrow, as interactive technologies become more and more commonplace, a lot of generally accepted ideas about employment and shift work will need to be revised or thrown out: in particular, the idea that the mass of wage-earners need to be concentrated in cities or urban outskirts, the **nodal** of international telecommunication networks substituting for the **central** of the cadastral organization of major cities.

Even though information processing has always been central to industrial management, it is clear that in the postindustrial era hyperconcentrated real-time computer systems are taking over from the traditional administration office. Today, when 'the office is made up of all the places you visit, in person, in thought, alone or with other people', the new corporate headquarters is no more than a node of networks set up to facilitate the transfer of information to dispersed commercial units, units which more often than not make their own decisions.[5]

We are thus seeing the commercialization of *multiple-user software* enabling simultaneous use by a set of subscribers to computer networks such as the **internet**, the World Wide Web of computer networks launched nearly fifteen years ago by the Pentagon.

At the same time, certain multinational firms strenuously encourage their employees to go and work *in the field* and only to touch down at home base for relatively short periods. These employees, known as 'mobile service providers', take their work with them wherever they go: to airports, on to planes, into cars or hotels, the underlying idea being that personnel should be out in the real world dealing with clients, rather than sifting through files at the office.

We are thus seeing a kind of fledgling 'business tourism' given a further boost by the growing practice of foisting 'subcontracting agreements' on certain executives who would otherwise find themselves out of a job. Armed with their telematic tackle, these executives set themselves up for a few hours or a few days at most in hotels, teleconferencing centres or on the stands of international exhibitions.

In the face of the 'teleconference' craze and the gradual decline of airline transport, one often hears the voice of temptation insinuating that one could probably 'do better business away from business', as though deterioration in neighbourly relations guaranteed commercial success![6]

Indeed, if the technologies of the electronic workplace free employees from the firm, the eight-hour day and the strictly geographic constraints of the factory will in turn become outdated social concepts. The actions and the places that tied employees and unions together and ultimately gave expression, a framework, to their different status in the hierarchy of industrial labour, will tomorrow look like outmoded rituals. But while the high level of mobility and the ubiquity of telecommuting certainly have their advantages, they also have a number of major drawbacks, in particular the fact that we can no longer draw a clear line between work and play, paid work now threatening to swamp all the private space and time we each thought we could do with as we pleased.

Finally, in this latest brand of a *Taylorism* that affects external rather than internal functions, each of the structures of the postindustrial firm has a precise role to play in production as well as in distribution and this, *under the constant time pressure of commercial or stock exchange events*, with hyperproductivity as the main objective.

Since the fragmentation of geographically scattered activities itself results from the instantaneous nature of commands, the problem is no longer so much one of organization of the real space and *local time* of the factory as of management of the real time of the *global space* of responsiveness to the orders of sleeping (silent) partners – the 'just-in-time' organization of postindustrial production imposing a pace that will soon require mass structural unemployment and the implementation of some kind of **global robotics** to satisfy the desire for super-responsiveness to the remote commands of a client base in future comprised of browsers, of channel surfers.

'*The effectiveness of electronic money lies in its mass, which increases its velocity of circulation*,' explain contemporary experts in an electronic stock trading system that more and more often generates a sort of 'virtual bubble' capable, if not of actually causing the market to crumble, then at least of inflicting cruel damage on the economic resources of a greater and greater number of countries. After *mass* and *energy*, this is the reign of *information*, reality's third dimension, bringing with it the incredible possibility of a new kind of shock: *information* shock, which all states are now trying to protect against since what it entails is the threat of a veritable 'coup d'état' fomented not by some two-bit political dictator but by the supreme tyranny of a computer system with the power totally to destabilize any state.[7]

Since real-time financial information is becoming more crucial than the money supply, even more essential than the *materiality* of the old gold standard, but also more essential than the *territoriality* of a nation's real space, how can we stay one jump ahead of regional geographic development when we go on refusing to think about democratic control of the way time is employed economically and politically, if not about actual time budgeting?

Just ahead of the future 'general accident' of the global economy, the United States, already possessing government bodies to take care of territorial security, has now created a body more specifically designed to ensure the economic security of its national interests in a bid to alleviate the damage done by *the technological fundamentalism of computer technologies*.

But let us return to the Old Continent. If the political will of the Europe of the Twelve (now Fifteen) is to see an initial programme of transcontinental transport networks in place as quickly as possible, what is the state of play with the very notion of territorial development? Can we still talk about some kind of geopolitics that would seriously commit the European Union to recovery of a *transnational* territory that is being dismembered, if not indeed turned into an agricultural desert? Or is the reverse the case: are they not, in fact, trying to hammer out a common 'metropolitics' designed further to increase the impact of the 'city network' on the country, thus concentrating the *unicity of time* of interurban transit to the detriment of the *unity of place* of the rural interval?

Everyone knows that if *distance* – all geographical distance – is currently yielding to the economic importance of *duration*, the problem of continental territorial development can no longer be framed so much in terms of organizing Europe's expanse, as in terms of the management of time: of that real time which dissolves the very reality of regional cultures, along with the particularities of the real spaces of those cultures. How else do we explain, for instance, European civil aviation's recent drop in air fares on international airlines and the contrasting increase on national services? Or again, the constant fall in the price of international telecommunications and the increase in regional rates?

Besides, at a time when international exchange time is *going global* and electronic highways are being opened up, ensuring urbanization of the real time of information transmission, surely we cannot fail to notice the parallel *virtualization of the real space* of regions, of countries, and the quasi-telluric contraction of the isochronous curves of Europe as a space, the Old Continent fading before the immateriality of 'telecontinents' built up of unending dataflows between Europe and America.

But let us get back to Europe's great engineering projects and the political significance of this initial programme of European infrastructural development. The whole point of all this development – the building of bridges and roadways, the digging of tunnels, the laying of railways and highways on expropriated land – is *to make the territory more dynamic*, in order to increase the transit speed of people and goods.

That great 'static vehicle' constituted by the road and railway networks promotes the acceleration of the small 'dynamic vehicles' that use them, allowing whole convoys to glide smoothly; and, pretty soon, resistance to the forward motion of mobile vehicles, shown, from time immemorial, by a nation's geographical depth, will disappear. But so will all topographical asperities, those hills and steep valleys that were the pride, the splendour, of the regions traversed, being ironed out. And the (sole) winner will be the outrageously outsized metropolitan agglomeration capable of absorbing, on its own, most of the power of the nations of Europe, along with a whole country's productive output. The current waning of institutional borders, echoing the decline of natural boundaries, will then be accompanied by the waning of the interval that once divided the peoples of Europe into nation states – to the great advantage of a city that is not so much *topical* and territorial as *teletopical* and extraterritorial. A city in which the geometric notions of urban centre and urban periphery will gradually lose their social significance, as 'left' and 'right' will lose theirs in the arena of political identity: in the age of the immateriality of *networks*, **communications** is gearing up to represent a possible alternative to the *party* politics of the age of immediate communication.

As an illustration of this phenomenon, which promotes both concentration and monopolization, we need look no further than a new Swiss project designed to replace the old 'intercity' rail network: the **Swiss metro**.

After the French high-speed trains and looking ahead to the future German Transrapid, the Swiss Confederation has just taken metropolitan logic to its natural conclusion by proposing to replace the old railway system with *an underground railway that will run at 400 kilometres per hour in a tunnel linking Switzerland's nine biggest cities.*

Moving under vacuum using magnetic suspension, and propelled by 'stators' (linear electric motors) fixed at various points along the tunnel walls, the **Swiss metro** will thus take up the 'electric canon' project originally dreamed up by the Germans at the end of the

Second World War. The explosive projectile initially intended to bombard England from the cliffs of the Pas-de-Calais will turn into *a subway train two hundred metres long*. Each of the cities thus linked will then lose its cantonal status to become one of the supersuburbs of a Switzerland suddenly transformed into a sort of 'capital to end all capitals', ultimately not so much political as metropolitical.

We might point out that, from the invention of the underground railway in the nineteenth century to this futuristic project largely inspired by the recent excavation of the Channel Tunnel, it has always been a matter of *clearing the surface of anything in the way*: too many carriages in Paris in the age of Fulgence Bienvenüe's Métro; today, with the **Swiss metro**, the mountain chain of the Alps!

Never smooth enough, never *desertified* enough, the solid element of the earth's surface seems from now on too restricting for transport acceleration. Hence the idea, this time on the part of the Italians, of unclogging the **autostrada**, with the launch of a series of Mediterranean car-ferry lines – **aquastrada** – running from north to south along the peninsula. Travelling at close to 100 kilometres per hour and barely grazing the surface of the liquid element, 'surface action' ships thus complement the 'tunnel action' of boring through the soil of Europe with high-speed rail links.

If we look at the latest developments in Formula One racing we see the same phenomenon at work. After the accident that caused the death of world champion Ayrton Senna, quite a few race tracks are now considered obsolete, their bends and surfaces making them too dangerous for such mega-powerful machines. Whence the pressure on promoters to come up with driver assistance in the form of vehicles remotely piloted from the stands. Formula One cars are fitted with a host of microprocessors that can save the driver from accidents caused by the effect of gravity, particularly on curves.

When even racing tracks are sealed off and ruled out of bounds as being too dangerous, after the example of the Imola track in Italy, we can be sure that all roads, all highways will soon become suspect and finally outmoded due to the deadly prowess of racing machines that are themselves no longer true 'automobiles', but test beds on wheels (back-up cars) designed to test engines on behalf of a car industry that is on the brink of crisis. *The auto-da-fé of automobiles at Imola* and the death of Ayrton Senna rang the death knell not only for the sinuous tracks of Europe (to the advantage of the more spectacular American tracks), but also for the *automotive car*, itself banned in town to the profit of *little electromotive cars*, veritable prostheses for spastics!

Some time ago, Antoine de Saint-Exupéry wrote, 'The aeroplane has taught us the straight line.' *Telematics will in future teach us the point, the inertia of the dead centre.*

The reign of the autonomous mobility of the household car is giving way to 'high-speed mass transit systems'. For us an era is ending, despite the construction of the European transcontinental transport network which will soon be under way; despite even the building of future motorways between Berlin and Warsaw, between Athens–Salonica and the Turkish border, between Lisbon and Valladolid.

Indeed, if geopolitics once required Roman roads or terrestrial motorways, the metropolitics that is taking shape will essentially require electronic information highways and satellite networks capable of achieving *unity of time* for a telecommunications system that is now universal. Along the lines of the **internet** network, originally designed to link up the firms of the American military-industrial complex, the new electronic highways will achieve general and instantaneous packet-switching, which will swiftly promote *global delocalization* of human activity. The former pre-eminence of the spatial situation will then gradually lose its historical importance, favouring temporary network access protocols using information routing to enable messages instantaneously transmitted long-distance to be connected.

So, the old *industrial and political* complex will be superseded by an *informational and metropolitical* complex, one associated with the omnipotence of the absolute speed of the waves conveying the various signals. Then, beyond the old **cosmopolis** modelled on ancient Rome, the world-city will surge forth, an **omnipolis** whose major clinical symptom is the stock exchange system, today computerized and globalized, generating as it does, at more or less constant intervals, *a virtual financial bubble* which is nothing less than the early-warning signal of the dire emergence of a new kind of accident, an accident no longer local and precisely located in space and time as before, but *a general global accident* which could well have radio-activity as its emblem.

To see if we can confirm this imminent *temporal homogenization* of a planet now subject to the tyranny of real time, that is to say, of a worldwide time that devalues the local time of immediate activity, let us take a look at a very recent project that should soon finish off the job of the time management practices of planetary telecommunications.

After opening up electronic information highways using fibre-optic cables to irrigate the full panoply of American metropolises, multimedia companies are gearing up to use technologies provided by President Reagan's 'Strategic Defense Initiative' to place in low Earth orbit more than 800 satellites designed to ensure coverage of the globe. The **Teledesic** project of Bill Gates and Greg McCaw, a veritable 'network to end all networks' which is capable of outperforming the **internet**, aims to rival **Motorola**'s further advanced, but less ambitious, **Iridium** project. Set up as a universal network, this awesome superstructure would then be leased to the different states, enabling their most isolated inhabitants to receive at home the whole array of telecommunication services, from telephony and tele-conferencing to instantaneous data transmission and telecommuting.

Note that once again *the constraint of terrestrial infrastructure is as intolerable as ever for the development of communication speeds.* Having in the course of history got rid of all kinds of unevenness from the world's surface, by flattening out pathways, roadways and highways, digging tunnels under mountains or under the sea to promote high-speed transport, they now find it necessary to do away with the constraint of the materiality of the information highway's buried cables. This is to be achieved through weightless satellites capable of spraying their radiations around over all the world's nations, the **infosphere** gearing up to rule tomorrow's **biosphere**.

It is ultimately in terms of this phenomenon of *desertification* and, especially, of growing *dematerialization* that we should measure the reality of European territorial development. Even though a second, more ambitious programme is on the European Union's agenda – one aimed at promoting, alongside the conveying of energy and information, the future control of the continent's environment – we should further specify that this globalization of information time implies an as yet unnoticed phenomenon of virtualization of the political. The virtual space of the telecommunications era is gearing up to take over from the geography of nations. And so, a new and final form of **cybernetics**, at once social and political, has emerged in the history of society. Our democracies have every reason to fear it.

Heraclitus warned, 'We must put out the excess rather than the fire.' This excess is currently the excessiveness of an economy that has become planetary; hence the drift of the European continent, now suffering the catastrophic effects of mass unemployment, teletechnologies no longer encouraging postindustrial firms to create jobs to improve their productivity, but to acquire new equipment, or even to relocate their production. *Global delocalization* is accompanied by a dislocation, a disintegration of the fabric of the corporate community in the name of a new law, not now of *proximity*, like that proper to the real space of a precisely located activity, but a law of *precariousness*, itself linked to the real-time interactivity of trade. This has reached the point where the *virtual company* that can exist independently of any productive collectivity and any geographical location is no longer a utopia. The conditions for its realization have already been tested by a firm as big as IBM, the multinational that is preparing to abandon its head office *to go and set up nowhere*!

So, alongside the development of leisure centres using techniques said to be those of virtual reality – those **cyberparks** that are springing up all over Japan and the United States, where visitors can submerge themselves in a cyberspace with which they enter into interaction – **virtual corporations** are also being designed that now register their productive activities exclusively in the **cyberworld** of real-time planetary trade. This leads to economic deregulation, if not indeed a veritable **social crash** – the inevitable result of the logic of production and distribution known as *just-in-time*, which forces each of the trading partners to do the rounds more and more often, faster and faster, covering the four corners of the globe. The *metropolitan sedentariness* of the employment pools thus makes way for an *omnipolitan nomadism* in which each employee, having become a 'subcontractor' against his will, is not so much a travelling salesman, a *particular individual*, as a *virtual particle* in a basically non-existent firm.

We now have a better idea of the nature of this **general accident** which threatens to strike the political balance of nations in attacking the global economy.

The *conjunctive proximity* of continental territorial development is today superseded by the *disjunctive precariousness* of worldwide time-management practices that provoke a sort of disintegration in the socio-political organization we have inherited from past centuries. The metaphor of nuclear catastrophe and fallout is no longer a stylistic trope, but in the end an accurate enough image of the damage to human *activity* caused by this sudden implosion-explosion of computerized *interactivity* which Albert Einstein predicted in the 1950s would probably constitute a second bomb, after the purpose-built atomic one.

PART 3

EYE LUST

'We should put the power of the human eye to use.'
Treinisch

Sight was once a cottage industry, an 'art of seeing'. But today we are in the presence of a 'tangible appearances business' that may well be some form of pernicious *industrialization of vision*.

What, in fact, is the true tree? The one perceived in a pause, every detail of which can be visually itemized, every branch and leaf; or the one glimpsed flashing past in the stroboscopic unfolding of the car windscreen, or else through the strange skylight of television?

On the response to such apparently meaningless questions a great number of practical consequences for daily life actually depend. If there is already no more photography in the sense in which its inventors, Niepce or Daguerre, practised it, but merely a *freeze frame*; and if, as a result, images frozen or arrested are now only 'stops' along the way of unfolding visual sequences, then we can look forward to a passion for gazing which will soon see the cottage industry of the amateur gaze giving up the ghost, making way for a vision industry based entirely on the motor, on the transceiver of those 'wave trains' that now carry video as well as radio signals. With the *automation of production* and now the transmission revolution rounding off the mobilizing effects of last century's transport revolution, we thus find ourselves in an age where *automation of perception of the world* is on the drawing board. As video maker Gary Hill puts it: 'Vision is no longer the possibility of seeing, but the impossibility of not seeing.'

The ban on representation in certain cultural practices and the refusal to see – women, for example, in the case of Islam – is being superseded at this very moment by the cultural obligation to see, with the overexposure of the visible of the age of image animation taking over from the underexposure of the age of the written word.

Is what we are seeing an optical or, more precisely, an opto-electronic fetishism? Should we avert our gaze, gingerly sneak a sidelong look, and so avoid the exploitative focus on offer? These are so many questions which are not exclusive to aesthetics but concern equally the *ethics of contemporary perception*.

I personally fear we are being confronted by a sort of pathology of immediate perception that owes everything, or very nearly everything, to the recent proliferation of photo-cinematographic and video-infographic *seeing machines*. Machines that by mediatizing ordinary everyday representations end up destroying their credibility.

'Not being able to believe your eyes' is no longer, in fact, a sign of amazement or surprise, but rather a mark of a 'conscientious objection' that now objects to the hold of the objective image, of the image mediatized not only by the live or recently pre-recorded TV broadcast, but also by an excessive *mobilization of public space* in which moving stairways and walkways are the missing link in the chain that leads from public transport's automobilization of the domestic household to the lift in the high-rise tower of the wired smart building.

So, the skyline that once limited the perspective of our movements is today joined by the square horizon of the TV set or the skylight of the plane or bullet train.

Since the optical unwinding of the reel now no longer lets up, it is becoming hard, even impossible, to believe in the stability of the real, in our ability to pin down a visible that never stops vanishing, the space of the building suddenly giving way to the instability of a public image that has become omnipresent.

In the face of this 'perceptual disorder' that affects each and every one of us, it might be appropriate to reconsider the ethics of common perception: are we about to lose our status as *eyewitnesses* of tangible reality once and for all, to the benefit of technical substitutes, prostheses for all seasons which will make of us the 'visually challenged', living off sight handouts, afflicted with a kind of paradoxical blindness due to overexposure of the visible and to the development of *sightless* vision machines, hooked up to the 'indirect light' of optoelectronics that now completes the 'direct optics' of sunlight or electricity?

Cinema means pulling a uniform over our eyes, warned Kafka. Today, with video and the digitized images of computer graphics, that threat is being borne out to such an extent that some sort of ethics committee on perception will soon be necessary. Without it we may well find ourselves going in for some kind of mad *eye training*, a subliminal *optically correct* conformism that will finish off the job of the conformism of *politically correct* language and writing.

Between habituation to unbelievably violent films and overuse of telescoping in televised sequences, we are already seeing a rhythmic dispossession of sight, due in particular to the growing ascendancy of the image and of sound. Tomorrow, if we are not careful, we will be the unwitting victims of a kind of conjuration of the visible, a visible doctored by wild acceleration of ordinary, everyday representations.

Studies on dyslexia recently conducted at Harvard University suggest that this affliction is less the product of a problem with language and more a kind of visual disorder. As a published report also indicates, this scientific finding corroborates the results of an Australian study revealing the clear tendency of dyslexics to see only one image at a time instead of the two the human eye normally perceives when images file past in the same direction or are run past at high speed. Will the acceleration of representations cause us to lose their *depth of field* and so impoverish our sight? The question remains unanswered, though it signals a grave problem for perception.

Finally, work in progress on digital image-processing, using algorithmic practices of 'visual reconstruction' necessary to the elaboration of *artificial vision*, seems to point to the fact that there could well exist a kind of *image energy* that would tend to keep to a minimum in the perceptual process just as, in physics, the dynamics of a process is often such that it evolves towards a state of equilibrium in which the energy is as low as possible.

Whatever the case may be with this kinematic energy that would complement kinetic and potential energies, the standardization of vision is on the agenda.

Let us take a look now at recent research on the ergonomics of perception. We know that several technologies exist to track eyes; some deploy optics, others use mechanical or electrical systems. Now, eye-tracking systems using electricity are almost universally adopted for human beings: 'Such a system is based on the fact that the eye is a polarized, binocular system whose electric dipole, when adjusted by direction of gaze to line of view, induces a periorbital electric field; the variations in this field caused by eye movements can be collected and amplified.'[1] The signal is either recorded or processed by computer to extract the parameters in a form adapted to specific requirements.

So the *oculometer* is used not so much as a means of testing whether an ocular system is healthy, but rather as a probe for discovering the precise moment when **stereographic** vision occurs. This is especially useful in improving data capture or 'keyboarding' in the pilot's **perceptual system**. This branch of ergonomic research has actually led, very recently, to new technology for replacing the instrument panel and its sundry indicator lights with a helmet, a sort of *virtual cockpit* whose transparent visor would display flight parameters at the precise moment these become indispensable, the rest of the time clearing the pilot's visual field of all signal interference.

Finally, since this type of fluctuating (real-time) optoelectronic display demands substantial improvement in human response times, delays caused by hand movements are also avoided by using both voice (speech input) and gaze direction (eye input) to command the device, *piloting no longer being done 'by hand' but 'by eye'*, by staring at different (real or virtual) knobs and saying **on** or **off** – this, thanks to *an infrared sensor that recognizes direction of gaze by scanning the back of the pilot's retina.*

Ophthalmology thus no longer restricts itself to practices necessitated by deficiency or disease; it has broadened its range to include an intensive exploitation of the gaze in which the depth of field of human vision is being progressively confiscated by technologies in which man is controlled by the machine: optoelectronic technologies that all have the aim of organizing the most subconscious visual reflexes in order simultaneously to improve the witnesses' reception of signals and their response times.

What is more, far from being satisfied with using retinal persistence alone, as formerly with the illusion created by the unwinding film reel, specialists in computer graphics imagery have now managed to *motorize sight*.

In the United States, for instance, we are seeing the use of *laser scanners* to improve the reality level of virtual world displays – Cyberspace. Note also the idea of replacing the miniaturized liquid crystal display screens of visualization helmets with laser microscanners: 'This system uses lasers employed in eye surgery that can safely scan low intensity laser beams directly onto the back of the retina and modulate colour images.'[2]

This practice of intrusion into the eye has the advantage of eliminating the bulky optical apparatus required to collimate virtual images, while producing extremely high quality visual sensations.

'*But can we still talk of* **images** *when there are no longer any* **pixels**, *the laser beam directly stimulating the retinal rods and cones of the eye?*'[3]

Faced with this sudden 'mechanization of vision', in which the *coherent* light impulse of a laser attempts to take over from the fundamentally *incoherent* light of the sun or of electricity, we may well ask ourselves what is the real aim, the as yet unavowed objective, of such instrumentalization – of a kind of *perception* no longer simply enhanced by the lenses in our glasses any more but by computer. Is it about improving the perception of reality or is it about refining reflex conditioning, to the point where even our grasp of how our perception of appearances works comes 'under the influence'?

After the *design of the object* and the serial aesthetic of industrial production and mass consumerism, it looks as though we are now going to see in the postindustrial era some sort of *design of moral standards*, an ocular reflex training regime in which the standardization of vision, denounced by Kafka not so long ago, will make way for a sort of *electro-ergonomic suppressant*, in which design of the pathways of waves and their sequential aesthetic will replace the movie theatre for the viewer armed with an audiovisual helmet that relays the eyeball's *mise en scène*, the optic nerve irradiated by laser beams reproducing on the screen of the occipital cortex that fine line of light once produced by the old movie projector.

There is no need to look any further for the reasons for the decline of the film industry: following on from the innovation of the earlier vision machines of photography, film or video, we are already seeing the beginnings of a true 'mechanization of perception', whereby the intrusion of optoelectronic devices right inside the nervous system partly explains the abandonment of projection rooms which have also become smaller and smaller.

A few years ago, on the occasion of the inauguration of the Géode, I wrote: 'Don't go to la Villette. Have no fear, the Géode will come to you.'[4] This premonition is now becoming a reality with virtual-world technology, the hemispherical rooms of the **Imax** or **Omnimax** model only ever being simulators of a spherical cinema to come: *eyeball cinema*.

We might observe that, here also, the electromagnetic transmission revolution paves the way for the transplantation *in vivo* of physiology-stimulating devices, the miniaturization practised by biotechnologies promoting implantation of postindustrial machinery into the living being's very insides. The pacemaker points the way to the coming insemination of *emotional prostheses* capable of adding to the pharmacological arsenal of stimulants and hallucinogens, physics quite clearly not wanting to let itself be outdone in this domain by chemistry!

Clearly, the increasing desertion of movie theatres is not a sign of a decline in 'cinematic obscurantism'. It is in fact the dawn of an 'infographic illusionism' that will, if we are not careful, wind up once again undermining the status of appearances, the reality principle of our immediate representations.

'*It is in the nature of the French not to like what they see.*'[5] Well, are they wrong or right? That is indeed the question: the question of choice in perception.

Are we free, truly free, to choose what we see? Clearly not. On the other hand, are we obliged, absolutely forced *against our will* to perceive what is first merely suggested then imposed on everyone's gaze? Not at all!

In the not so distant past the spectacle of the world was limited, if that is the word, to the rhythm of the seasons, the alternation of night and day over the changing horizon of the landscape. But now the prevailing rapid transport and transmission technologies have managed to *mobilize* our field of perception non-stop – not only within the artificial construct of the metropolis, but within the expanse of whatever vast territories are traversed thanks to the feats of earthbound or airborne motors.

How can we resist this deluge of visual and audiovisual sequences, the sudden *motorization of appearances* that endlessly bombard our imagination? Are we still free to try and resist the ocular (optic or optoelectronic) inundation by looking away or wearing sunglasses? Not out of modesty any more or because of some religious taboo, but out of a concern to preserve one's integrity, one's *freedom of conscience*.

In cartography and elsewhere, animation serves in the waging of war; it is also used nowadays to defeat the peacefulness of the everyday environment.

At a time when everyone is rightly asking about the *freedom of expression* and the political role of the media in our society, it would surely be a good thing if we also asked ourselves about the individual's *freedom of perception* and the threats brought to bear on that freedom by the industrialization of vision and of hearing – noise pollution being doubled more often than not by a discreet pollution of our vision of the world through the sundry tools of communication.

Surely it would then be appropriate to entertain a kind of *right to blindness*, just as there is already a right to relative deafness or, at least, to a lowering of the noise level in shared space, public places. Should we not insist on an immediate lowering of intensity in the transmission of appearances? Information theory could enlighten us, it would seem, about the damage done by regular increases in the dose of sequences to the meaning, the significance of our immediate environment.

If desire to know the world has today been left behind by the need to exploit it, shouldn't we try to limit the extreme exploitation of the optical layer of tangible reality, as we do elsewhere – for example, with ecology? Sometimes all you have to do is look differently to see better.

Can we really just go on forgetting about the need for a science of the iconic environment, for an 'ecology of images', when every kind of extreme pollution of natural substances reaches us more often than not through the mass media?

If, according to Kafka, cinema means pulling a uniform over your eyes, television means pulling on a straitjacket, stepping up an eye training regime that leads to eye disease, just as the acoustic intensity of the walkman ends in irreversible lesions in the inner ear.

We might add that rejection of visual (audiovisual) conformism would also tend to rule out establishing some kind of *optically correct politics* which could cause the manipulation of sight by future mass communication tools quickly to take on totalitarian overtones.

By way of illustrating what I am saying about the need for an ethics of perception, here is the 'eye' witness account of Wubo J. Ockels, the European astronaut who went into orbit with the Americans: 'What I felt personally was like going back to, or having a vision of, the village where you were born. *You don't want to live there any more* because you've grown up and moved away and now you'd rather live the life of the city. But it moves you as "Mother Earth"; *you just know you wouldn't want to go back and live with her.'*

Vision of *planet-man*, in which the eyeball of the weightless witness observes the old terrestrial globe with a kind of sovereign scorn; vision of a lost world linked to the *Weltschmerz* of the nihilism of Western technology.

★

'*To command, you must first of all speak to the eyes,*' as Napoleon
Bonaparte pointed out. Indeed, to intimate an order to a subordinate
is always to intimidate his gaze. Like a reptile fascinating its prey, any
command rules out the free will of the person for whom it is meant.
Hence the importance of sight, much more than of hearing, in that
military discipline that is an army's main strength.

Let us look now at recent developments in weapons research and
technological feasibility studies. Apart from the space technology
programmes that have been top priority since 1991, the bulk of
research initiated by the French Defence Ministry in 1992 involves
optoelectronics, computer science and robotics – but biology and the
social sciences feature too.

A few examples selected at random will reveal the general outlook
of the Conseil de recherches et études de défense (Committee for
Defence Research and Studies). Under the heading 'Biology and
Ergonomics', we read: 'Within the framework of signal modelling
and processing in biology, a study of the three-dimensional cerebral
localization of electrical activities using surface scanners has been
assigned to university X in Brittany. Among the practical applications,
one may cite localization of the frontal lobe sites where information
is processed, as well as localization of the sources of epilepsy.'

Later, under the heading 'The Man–Machine Interface', we also
read: '*In the ergonomics sector, a study of the organization of displays within
the pilot's visual space* has been assigned to laboratory Y. If we want to
better adapt a pilot's perceptual aids, we need to enhance use of perception of "relief", which is originally binocular, by developing *a
working model of the third dimension.*'

Let us take another area of military research: **lasers**. Modern
weapons systems rely more and more on rangefinders with laser sensors for greater accuracy in sighting: '*Studies of the physiology of the eye
have recently shown that there exist wavelengths to which the eye is less vul-
nerable.* As a result, company Z is studying a laser rangefinder with
added safety.'

Finally, by way of confirming the exponential development of 'scanners' and other 'sensors' in microelectronics, we also read, in the file headed 'Computer and Robotic Systems': 'Within the context of work on neuronal machines, the Institut d'électronique fondamentale (Institute of Basic Electronics) at Orsay is conducting *studies on the retina, on a retinal light receptor cell that may be capable of implementing neuronal algorithms of shape recognition.*'[6]

These are all so many examples of the strategic importance of the visual display, of a computer-assisted vision in which the eyeball gradually becomes the object of military-industrial development, just as the discovery and conquest of the terrestrial globe were once the object of the great military conquerors.

With ocular intrusion now superseding the invasion of vanquished countries, how can we fail to foresee the abrupt decline of geopolitics in favour of a sort of **iconopolitics**, in which the reign of the image would soon be concerned not so much with multiplying recording surfaces or screens, as with the discreet, 'furtive' invasion of the time depth of our field of vision?

As the big screens of movie houses yield little by little to the small screens of domestic television, the way things will go in the future is now clearly signposted: despite the boom in panoramic screens for instantaneous television broadcasting in stadiums and other places, the real action lies elsewhere, in the imminent nano-technological miniaturization of integrated circuits that will promote the *iconic insemination of 'consumer' information*, not so much *in situ*, as previously, but *in vivo*, with the grafting of visual interference rounding off the implanting of organs and sundry prostheses.

When public health experts are already predicting that in the year 2000: '*half of all surgical operations performed will involve organ transplants and implants of prostheses*', surely we cannot fail to see that the *site* of cutting-edge technologies is no longer so much the territorial body,

the geographic expanse of our world proper, for so long rigged out
with the most cumbersome infrastructures (canals, bridges and roadways, telegraph lines, etc.), but now well and truly man's animal body,
the body proper of an individual who will soon be subject to the
reign of biotechnology, of nanomachines capable not only of *coloniz-
ing* the expanse of the world, but also the very thickness of our
organisms.

Let us now take a look at the new development in eye micro-
surgery of using endoscopy. For some years now, use of endoscopy
in eye surgery has been spreading thanks to the endoscope's minia-
ture probes which are inserted in the eye, equipped with a video
camera. As an example, the ophthalmology technology market has
just seen the launch of *a new type of apparatus called the* **polycam**. *The*
polycam *consists of a probe 1.7 millimetres in diameter, a light generator,
a computer and a video scanner, enabling intra-ocular structures to be reproduced on a screen.* It is hoped that it will not be long before this
micro-endoscope incorporates *laser fibres and instrument channels that
will provide both a visual display tool and a surgical scalpel simplifying
manipulation.*[7]

We have come a long way from the huge recording cameras that
used to be set up in television studios, or from the **Omnimax** projector with its great reels in the Géode at the Parc de la Villette. *The
microcamera penetrates right into the patient's eye*, an eye that then
becomes both the theatre of all kinds of special effects, as we have
already seen, and the theatre of various manipulations. Witness, on
the occasion of the tenth European Congress of Cataract Surgeons
meeting in Paris in September 1992, the presentation of a new
system that will soon be able to replace glasses and contact lenses in
the correction of eye problems: the **laser excimer** is a laser that can
this time *sculpt the deficient cornea with micrometric precision.* A kind of
'plastic surgery' that puts the knife into eyesight, rather than into a
nose or the old double chin; in future, a facelift will not be about the

beauty of a face; it will be about correcting the individual's image and field of vision. They call this new type of operation **photo-ablation**.

Note also that what is happening to the presentation of the object is now happening to ocular representation: **design** no longer involves design of the material forms the finished product will take so much as design of information and of various stimuli. It is just a small step from the *multimedia* screen object to the *metadesign* of computer-assisted perception and on to plastic surgery for *optically correct* eyesight. To imagine that step will never be taken stems from an illusion no longer optical but aesthetic!

Indeed, at a time when more than 90 per cent of micro-electronic production is engaged in the manufacture of discrete components (scanners, sensors, detectors) and when they are cooking up – for the human organism this time – 'smart pills' capable of instantaneously transmitting information on an individual's nervous function, surely we cannot go on denying the probability of some form of *neurotech-nological processing of mental imagery*.

We should remind those who might still be in some doubt about this 'technoscientific' drift that the way the brain processes complex information remains one of the major stumbling blocks for the neurosciences: a recent study at Oxford University argues that the information coding necessary to recognize a face, for instance, is done at the level of a small number of neurones, a few dozen at most.[8] This low-level series obviously favours future discoveries concerning the coding processes of mental imagery.

For two years now, we have also been seeing renewed interest on the part of neurophysiologists in questions concerning *the temporal aspect of information processing*, the time depth of the stimulus prevailing over depth of field and the study of the different zones of a visual cortex that has now apparently become perfectly familiar.[9]

One last confirmation of the imminent development of mental imagery **meta-design**: at the 'Design 92' symposium hosted by the Research Ministry, the concept of *spun optical fibres* opened up a vast number of applications, in particular in the area of optoelectronic systems of measurement, involving both the automobile – with the manufacture of *hypovigilance-sensing in the steering wheel* – and computer science, with the construction of optical keyboards that do away with the analogue model. Let us hope that, for want of 'hypervigilance', we are never totally devoid of vigilance regarding the ethics of immediate perception.

FROM SEXUAL PERVERSION TO SEXUAL DIVERSION

'They think they are happy because they are not moving.'

Tristan Bernard

With cybersexuality, you no longer divorce, you disintegrate. Proprioceptive reality suddenly becomes improper; it is all done with reciprocal distancing.

So, what is being set up is a discreet, furtive conjunction not based on attraction any more but on mutual rejection and repulsion. Thanks to copulation between partners who are already no longer 'joined together', the aesthetics of disappearance is in turn vanishing in the face of the ethics of the essential disappearance of one's 'nearest and dearest' – the spouse, the lover – to the benefit of this 'furthest' (and not so dear) that Nietzsche once urged us to love.

After the seduction of simulation comes the disappointment of substitution: the woman-object of all desire, all fantasy, suddenly yields to the *object-woman*. This inversion, the symptom of a vast explosion of tangible reality, is merely the effect of crossing the 'time barrier'; the barrier of this limit-time of the speed of electromagnetic light-waves that disqualifies not only the relative speed of the living being but all matter, all effective presence of other people. The result is a panic-stricken disjunction already clearly demonstrated by the scale of divorce and the exponential growth of single-parent families. To prefer the virtual being – at some remove – to the real being –

close-up – is to take the shadow for the substance, to prefer the metaphor, the clone to a substantial being who gets in your way, who is literally on your hands, a flesh-and-blood being whose only fault is to be there, here and now, and not somewhere else.[1]

The great mutation of remote-action teletechnologies will, in fact, only have helped tear us away from the dimensions of the world as we know it. Whether steam engine (train) or combustion engine (automobile, aeroplane), the acceleration of techniques of propulsion will have caused us to lose touch with tangible reality. The aviator waxes nostalgic: 'The plane tears you away, makes you live dangerously, offers you happiness, brings you back when it's good and ready! The plane is the only thing I've ever really loved' (Claude Roy).

At the foot of the wall of time, of this *global* time that has superseded *local* time, there is indeed another explosion, another supersonic **bang** that signals the loss of reality of the man or woman one none the less claims to be meeting up with or to love.

As with the nozzle on the jet engine of a machine capable of breaking the sound barrier, everything comes together in long-distance love, thanks to the power of ejecting others, to this ability to ward off their immediate proximity, to 'get off on' distance and make headway in sensual pleasure the way jet propulsion propels the jet. So, just as the supersonic aircraft's take-off enables it to *overfly* Mother Earth and the geography of the continents, so the 'remote manipulation' of jet-propelled love allows partners to *overcome* their reciprocal proximity without risk of contamination, the electromagnetic prophylactic outdoing by a long shot – and how! – the fragile protection of the condom.

What was till now still 'vital', copulation, suddenly becomes optional, turning into the practice of remote-control masturbation. At a time when innovations are occurring in artificial fertilization and genetic engineering, they have actually managed also to interrupt coitus, to short-circuit conjugal relations between opposite sexes, with the aid of biocybernetic (teledildonic) accoutrements using sensor-effectors distributed over the genital organs.

'*The deepest thing in man is his skin,*' Paul Valéry once claimed. This is where the very latest perspective comes in: the *tactile perspective* of so-called 'touching at a distance' (tactile telepresence), which now puts the finishing touches on the classic perspectives of sight and hearing. And we cannot begin to understand the outrageousness of cybersexuality without this *paradoxical cutaneous perspective*.

In donning the DataSuit, *the individual slips into information*; his body is suddenly endowed with a second skin, with a muscle and nerve interface that fits over his own cutaneous layer. For him, for both of them, information becomes the sole 'relief' of corporeal reality, its unique 'volume'.

With this 'overwear', literally woven out of electronic impulses coding and decoding each of their emotions, partners in virtual love engage in a cybernetic process in which the operator console is no longer satisfied just to synthesize images or sounds. From now on, it orchestrates sexual sensations.

We have had *chemical suppressants*, psychotropic drugs. Here is the *electronic suppressant* – only, the desired effect is the reverse. It is now no longer a matter of damping down a momentary madness, but of whipping madness up, driving it to a frenzy. And this frenzy is contagious, transmitted instantaneously. They say that old priest of the American psychedelic movement, Timothy Leary, made long-distance love with a Japanese woman living in Tokyo.

At the heart of this cyberculture, the same old law operates as always in the technical arena: the *law of least action*.

After the transport revolution, which once promoted the honeymoon in Venice or somewhere, the age of the revolution in *amorous transport* is upon us, largely fostered by the development of the tools of the instantaneous transmission revolution.

The virtual consummation of the *act of the flesh* being to turned-on couples what the virtual community already is to a lay society of

internet subscribers, we will in the near future see a phenomenal divorce rate.

Indeed, if industrial technologies have progressively favoured the decline of the *extended* family of the rural world and promoted the *bourgeois*, and then the *nuclear*, family (so aptly named) at the time of last century's urban expansion, the end of the supremacy of physical proximity in the megalopolis of the postindustrial age will not content itself with promoting a boom in the *single-parent* family. It will go on to provoke an even more radical gap between men and women, thereby directly threatening the future of sexual reproduction. Parmenides' great divide between masculine and feminine principles will widen further as a result of the very performance of love at a distance.

Let us turn now to the reasons for the amazing privileging of sexual reproduction in the evolution of animal species, when partheno-genesis seemingly offered a more economical alternative. At the end of a long project, Doctors Stephen Howard and Curtis Lively of Indiana University have recently come to the conclusion that 'the commingling of genes which all sexual reproduction implies allows the risk of extinction to be reduced to a minimum where species are faced with various infections, but especially, where they are faced with predictable mutations of the species.' Now, there is just one single mutation that nature overlooked: the mutation of bio-technology.

With the development of the technosciences of the living organism – research on the human or procreant genome – which we are seeing today, the biosphere and the technosphere are merging thanks, on the one hand, to the feats of nanotechnologies, and to those of computer science, on the other; and we can only expect further drifts before too long, further noisy mix-ups in genetic information.

One of the most amazing examples of this is not the *test tube baby* of in vitro fertilization but in fact, and sooner than you think, *love experienced at a distance*, thanks to telesexual interactivity.

We are here touching (so to speak!) on a paradox which consists in our *coming together at a distance* in future for exchange.

Let us examine for a moment what is lost, or at least in danger of being completely forgotten, in the practices of cybernetic sexuality, which even threatens to attack sexual reproduction itself, the desire for procreation already largely cauterized by our way of life.

Today, if immediate proximity is still clearly defined by *being here present*, tomorrow this situation risks becoming dangerously blurred or actually disappearing, taking with it the old rule of socializing: *You can tell a man by the company he keeps.*

But before going any further, we need to go back a moment over the role of mating dances in the animal kingdom and the courtship manoeuvres and 'engagements' that were once the prelude to 'nuptials' between spouses who would then 'found a line' with their offspring.

Traditionally, weddings were marked, on the one hand, by the voyage, the auspicious distancing that either preceded or followed the ceremony, and so kept alive the memory of the biological risks of the spouses' possible consanguinity.[2] And, on the other hand, by the actual *act of the flesh*, a coupling which guaranteed that the marriage had indeed been consummated, copulation ensuring the legal reality of the contract.

But now nuptial rites are in turn feeling the impact of a way of life in which rushing around prevails over any reflection, to the point where, in the United States most notably, the popularity of the 'express marriage' clearly signals that future weddings will privilege the voyage over the 'wedding ceremony': the accelerated nomadism of the *drive-in marriage* will soon be outdone by a *virtual marriage* along the lines of what happened in 1995 at the Salon de l'Institut National de l'Audiovisuel in Monte Carlo, where telespouses exchanged their vows, decked out in video headgear and DataSuits.

From now on, distancing prevails over nuptial abduction; as, with tele-conferencing, what counts above all is the separation, the putting asunder of face-to-face parties; touch, physical contact between partners, being no longer the go so much as the rejection of the other person.

Hence the development of *sex tourism* and the setting up, here too, of worldwide child prostitution networks, as in Thailand, where this brand of *sexual diversion* represents more than 80 per cent of national revenue.

A bit like extreme mountaineering, where scaling a summit now counts less than how fast you can race across the mountain on a trail bike, sexual practices are preparing to **diverge**.

Like a reactor that can no longer keep up its production of nuclear energy and gears up to explode, *the couple that was the driving force* of history is entering divergence mode and gearing up to vanish into the ether. So much so that mutual repulsion is already winning out over attraction, over sexual seduction.

So, it is easy to see why there is such a sharp rise in *sexual harassment* complaints in the United States, why more and more women are bringing 'legal proceedings on the basis of alleged intentions' at the precise moment when the vogue in serial divorces has given way to a vogue in the series decay of the generator couple.

Despite appearances, this has nothing to do with morals or the permissive nature of postmodern society, since what we have here is chiefly a technological and anthropological phenomenon of unknown magnitude.

Potentially to be able to substitute a discrete *media-generated* discon-nection for the immediate connection of bodies thanks to cybersex's bag of tricks is to trigger a process of *physiological and demographic dis-integration* without precedent in history.

Far from reproducing the usual dichotomy between the pleasure of the senses – the art for art's sake of the sex act - and the act of the flesh intended to engender family descendants, the teletechnologies of remote love are inaugurating not only a furtive form of *remote birth control*, but also the beginnings of a *hyperdivorce* that will eventually endanger the future of human begetting.

Leonardo Sciascia warned: 'When you lose sight of the facts anything can happen.' If the *virtual pleasure* of sexual telepresence were eventually to outstrip the *real pleasure* of embodied love, as is probable, soon the only societies left to ensure the continuation of the human race will be those that are underdeveloped and, worse, 'media'-deprived.

After having laid off call-girls, hot on the heels of 'streetwalkers', the cybernetics of future sex hotlines will shortly make redundant the male and female of a totally disqualified human race, to the advantage of the sex machines of media masturbation.

'The individual of the scientific age is losing his capacity to experience himself as a *centre of energy*,' observed Paul Valéry, applying his intuition to a little-explored area, that of the animate, of the movement that drives the living being. Indeed, the movement of living organisms remains an enigma: the enigma of life itself. 'Batting your eyelids, contracting your muscles or picking up speed if you're a runner all seem to emanate spontaneously *from within*, unlike the motion of a truck, a plane or a rocket, where the driving force comes from the sudden expansion of gas at high temperature; unlike, also, the motion of a sailing boat, of waves or even trees stirring in the wind, since movement here is imposed by external elements.'[3]

As sources of energy, vital organisms accordingly behave like 'biomolecular' complexes transforming light or chemical energy into whatever is necessary to life: motion, heat or inner equilibrium. But this *metabolic* transformation was until now tangible, psychologically speaking, the egocentration of living persons being identified not only with their health, but with their 'form', their being in top form in the morning, for instance, when the nerve impulses wake up and *wake us up*.

How do we interpret admission of defeat by someone like Valéry here? This loss that we anxiously sense within ourselves and around us, with the spread of passivity? Is it premature ageing due to stress, to living at a pace that overloads our reflexes and diminishes *proprioceptive* reflexion? Most likely. But there is another explanation, an *exteroceptive* one that concerns the different ways of driving the vehicles that convey us and aid us more and more frequently in our travels, our excursions.

Again, as I pointed out in an earlier work, it is revealing to consider the historic evolution of the various 'drivers' cabins'.[4] In the recent past, for instance, one drove in the open air, in contact with the atmosphere, listening to the sound of the engine and the wind, and feeling the cell of the machine vibrate; but today excessive speed has contributed to the driver's being gradually shut away, initially behind the screen of his goggles, then behind the windscreen and finally, *right inside the sedan*.

Pioneers drove 'by instinct'; this gave way to driving 'by instrument' and then to 'automatic' steering, to say nothing of the remote-control piloting which an unbelievable assortment of machines have these days.

How can we fail to see that the love relationship will suffer exactly the same fate, with the cybernetic steering of disunited lovers? The remote piloting of sensations and so of physical enjoyment will one day soon echo the loss of contact with the body of that voluptuous 'speed machine' that envelops the driver so closely that an expert, Ayrton Senna, once claimed he not only slipped into his flame-proof Formula One driver's bodysuit, *but that he also literally put on his racing car*.

With the body's loss of a sense of its own energy, what is being played out, in a word, is a whole new episode in the history of prosthetics which is a history of debilitation, to put it mildly. In the view of Leroi-Gourhan for one, tools or instruments of any kind were supposed to extend man's organs, as with the fist improved by the hammer, the hand by pliers or tongs, and so on. This is not too hard to swallow in relation to *mechanics*, but it loses all credibility when we move from the notion of *mass* to the notion of *energy* (in particular, electrical energy) and, particularly, to the notion of *information* as the third dimension of matter. Indeed, when *mechanical relays* yield to *electrical relays* the break becomes obvious: the body gets disconnected so completely that the electromagnetic impulses of the new *remote control* end, with channel surfing, for instance, in the behavioural inertia of the individual; the law of least action finally winds up in cybersexuality, pulling the plug on the animate being of the Lover.

With 'biomechanical' *extension* on the one hand and 'energy' ablation on the other, the individual of the technoscientific age effectively loses the capacity to *experience himself* as a centre of energy; he becomes useless and will eventually become totally superfluous when faced with the *automation* of his productive and perceptual functions.

'Only a new way of getting pleasure can save us,' declares one of cyberculture's advertising slogans.

In a very short poem on acceleration, Saint-Pol Roux put this desire well, speaking of transport:

'Going faster is playing with death.

Going even faster is getting off on death.'[5]

This hits the nail on the head as far as the capabilities of instantaneous transmission go.

With zoophilia now bowing out before the nascent technophilia of long-distance love, so begins 'the game of love and chance', a game of pathological inertia bound up with the triumph of comfort and emotional self-sufficiency.

'For whoever has understood that he is mortal, the pangs of death begin,' observed Arthur Schnitzler. To get off, if not on death itself, then at least on the death throes of its virtual presence, on a gradual paralysis of one's faculties, is indeed the as yet unavowed stake of 'teleoperations', in which divided lovers are no longer there together except via their respective remote controls, the ghost of the emission-reception of an energy signal now replacing orgasm. Games of reciprocal electrocution of which laboratory rats once had a little foretaste before going under the knife.

By way of comparison, let us look at another kind of death rattle of presence in the world: Alzheimer's disease, the senile dementia that affects the tangible reality of the subject.

Cut off from a body that has become independent from his mind, *the victim is not there for anyone, not even for himself.*

Unconscious, subject to irreversible memory lapses and to spatial and temporal disorientation, he *ceases to exist in the here and now*, only occasionally to wake up completely out of sync with his environment, no matter how hard nursing staff may try to offer a few spatiotemporal pointers in the patient's brief periods of alertness to force him, if only for a moment, to maintain some connection with his body, some relationship with those around him.

At the precise moment when reality is not what it was, the victim escapes to a world of his own in a pathological virtuality not dissimilar to the *cyberpathology* of divided lovers, skilled players of an interactive game that keeps them apart, in the middle of a virtual space that no one but they will ever know. *Cybernauts* of a precocious dementia, that enables each one of us to plug into any network whatsoever where *sexual harassment* is not only tolerated, but actively encouraged (by subscription), 'telesexual' decentralization cleverly completing that of the electronic workplace.

★

Sex no longer exists; it has been replaced by fear.

Fear of the other, of the dissimilar, has won out over sexual attraction. After the struggle against the gravity of weighty bodies and all the research done on techniques of levitation and weightlessness, there begins a similar war on that universal attraction that enables the species to survive: genetic engineering, artificial fertilization and so on are all permutations of the same assault on the living being.

'If the act of procreation were neither the outcome of a desire nor accompanied by feelings of pleasure, *but a matter to be decided on the basis of purely rational considerations, is it likely the human race would still exist?*' asks Schopenhauer in his essay on the metaphysics of love.[6]

A century later, cybernetic research into sexual hijacking once again poses the question of knowing where this separation of bodies, this *diastase* of the living, will land us.

After the various 'unnatural' *perversions*, new alternative practices of love are emerging: complex *diversions* these, no longer 'animal' and zoophile, but 'mechanical' and blatantly technophile.

But what really lurks behind this panic-stricken withdrawal, this retreat, before the act of the flesh? Fear of catching AIDS or other fears, other, disavowable, terrors?

Mysteriously, the science of machines exiles us both from the geophysical world and from the physical body of another who always contradicts my ego and whose vital necessity is a mere shadow of what it once was in the age when the reign of the animal in all its energetic power still dominated the *synthetic*, or rather *surrogate, energies* that have since carried the day.

Defeat of the facts before the proliferation of information, itself *synthezised* to an incredible degree by mass communication tools, in which the image is already more important than the thing which it is never anything more than an 'image' of. But also – and this is what matters to us here – *defeat of the fact of making love*, here and now, to the benefit of a mechanical medium in which 'distance' once more becomes *distentio*, distension and dissension between partners, the game of love and chance becoming a vulgar *parlour game*, a sort of virtual casino, not unlike the stock exchange where, on those celebrated *derivatives markets*, traders and other golden boys amuse themselves breaking the bank the whole year long.

Here is Schopenhauer again on the subject of sexual interest – forgetting financial interest for the moment – apropos the coming cybernetic monopolization of sensual pleasure: 'This interest, which is the source of all commerce in love, from the most passing fancy to the most serious passion, remains for each of us the truly great affair, the one whose success or failure touches us most keenly, from which it derives the name, par excellence, of "love affair".'[7]

Imagine for a moment that the oldest profession in the world were to become the biggest 'multinational' there is; better still, that the consumer society, looking beyond the products currently available at the supermarket, were shortly to turn into a telesexual consumer society. The multimedia world would no longer just be the casino so loudly decried by economists but an actual brothel, a **cosmic brothel**, the startling commercial success of the sex hotline repeating itself ad infinitum thanks to the prowess of interactive telecommunications.

But another aspect of the emergence of sexual diversion becomes clear, reinforced as it is by the maniacal individualization that, with the demographic crisis, threatens our society. As we all know from experience of our own relative lack of philanthropy: '*The intensity of love is tied to a very obstinate selectivity*.'[8] So conditions of life in the world-city, with the decline in the family as a unit, will further accelerate the self-sufficiency of the hardened celibate, thereby bolstering the quest for intensity, 'extreme sports' more and more frequently finding their equivalent in the search for high-risk sexual experiences.

Indeed, if the existence of the social body patently comes before the existence of the animal body that it generates, and if 'being per se resides in the species more than in the individual', contemporary individuation menaces the persistence of being at every turn.[9]

'Well, what other subject could be of greater interest than that which touches on the good or the bad of the species? *For the individual is to the species what the surface of the body is to the body itself.*'[10]

Surface still, not so long ago, with the incomparable depth of the skin (Valéry); **interface** today, thanks to the performance of telecommunication between bodies **indivi** which achieves the paradox of a **totalitarian individualism** by enabling not only 'remote union' (teleconferencing), but also the telesexual union of genital sensations; **hyperdivorce** for a humanity united in its very disunity, whereby *interactivity* produces a disintegration of bodies analogous to the disintegration of the elementary particles of matter caused by *radioactivity*.

It is hard to resist comparing Schopenhauer to Heidegger here. According to Heidegger, technology *really* accomplishes metaphysics; but *cybernetics* will *virtually* achieve the 'metaphysics of love' – to the detriment of the species and its sexual reproduction.

'**Cyberfeminism** participates in the development of a feminist consciousness and emphasizes the importance of the multimedia in perception of the body.'[11] With these words a new group begins its manifesto. Taking up the terms of an article that appeared in *Socialist Review* ten years ago, the women's collective continues: 'Communication technologies and biotechnologies *are important tools that enable us to reinvent our bodies* . . . The emergence of postindustrial culture is going to entail a profound change in human societies. *Similarly, the sensory and organic architecture of the human body, sexual and cultural identities, indeed our modes of thinking, and the place each of us occupies will be modified.*'

Further extending this statement of the obvious political and cultural importance of **cyberspace** in moral liberation, the author finally poses the key question of control: '*Who will in future generate* *the codes and the specifications by which bodies will be represented in cyber-space where everything exists as metaphor?* This already depends on the manner in which cybernauts choose to engage with the virtual body.'

Cyberfeminism then weighs in with the big question of political responsibility in the construction of such a body, 'a truly revolution-ary subject': 'What will happen to the social relationships of sexuality, the body's sexual modes of communicating, desire and sexual differ-ence in the age of the coded metaphor? *Control of interpretation of the body's boundaries is a truly feminist issue.*'

As one can readily appreciate, at a time when the boundaries between biology and technology, man and the machine, are being effaced one by one, it is simply high time we took a fresh stand. Hence the final appeal: 'It is urgent that women participate in the construction of cyberspace by developing a **cyberimaginary** capa-ble of becoming a tool of their own self-construction. If it is true that the multimedia can be a formidable instrument of control and sub-jugation, it is up to us women to turn it into a tool of emancipation.'

Much more than a manifesto of militant feminism, this text already has the ring of a cry of alarm in the face of a mechanical sur-rogacy that would supplant the carnal attractions of femininity. Despite a whole host of surrogates for sexual organs (vibrators, dildos), simulation has in fact already ceased to be viable since it is itself about to be given a new twist through 'alternative' practices in which the hyperrealism of the virtual body would be to the flesh what drugs are to the mind – a deadly addiction to narcotics herald-ing what will, in the near future, become the implacable imaginary of **cybersex**.

'**Speed: the coitus of the future**' prophesied, over half a century ago, Saint-Pol Roux, the surrealist specialist in a living cinema capable of engendering a human race full of spectators: '*O camera womb, dare to really give birth! Flattened images, swell into relief! Make* those French letters reek of sex, breathe life into all those hollow windbags.'[12]

Today, it is in the can. Thanks to the force-feedback control glove (DataGlove) and, especially, to the DataSuit, *everything is ruled by lightning*, and the *coup de foudre* of disunited lovers suddenly becomes a *coup de grâce*. From erotic entertainment we then move on to sexual diversion and shortly to a fatal divergence – that of the reactor that sets off nuclear fission.

It's a very thin line between *ecstasy* and *diastase* for, in future, it is at the speed of electromagnetic radiation that cybernetic orgasm will occur.

In effect, if distancing brings (interactive) lovers together to the point where they manage *to love those far-off as they do themselves*, the gap between the wedding and the divorce will have been closed once and for all.

By way of a provisional conclusion, let us review the early ethical reactions to this telematic mutation in sexuality. In an apostolic letter published in 1994, in honour of the International Year of the Family, Pope John Paul II declared: 'Union and procreation cannot be *artificially* separated without altering the intimate truth of the conjugal act itself.'[13]

Far from chiming in as a simple rejection of contraception or the usual repetition of the indissoluble nature of the bonds of marriage, this statement points to another major question: the question of the nature of the separating **artefact**. What *artificial construct* are we in fact talking about when even bodily union is eclipsed by a virtual tele-sexuality that advocates the *separation of bodies* and no longer just divorce?

What happens not only to the future of holy matrimony, but also to divorce, when they are now literally dissolving, not the *couple*, but *copulation*?

More recently still, at a congress held in Rome in the spring of 1995, experts from the Catholic Church launched an appeal against the all too predictable development of cybernetic love. Denouncing such interactive practices as a 'catastrophe for love', the Roman contingent noted that the sex industry now offers lovers *'an illusory and artificial space, an easy way out of people's inability to deal with each other responsibly'*, and that the best of all possible worlds of the remote consummation of sex with one or more partners is never anything but a denial of human coupling, being no longer merely an accident of marriage, like adultery or divorce, but a denial of the very reality of the 'act of the flesh' and so of true knowledge of the other for, in biblical terms, *to know the other is to love him*.[14]

As we have seen, the 'information revolution' that has today superseded the revolution in industrial manufacturing is not without danger, for the damage done by progress in **interactivity** may well be as harmful in the future as that done by **radioactivity**. The 'computer bomb' previously denounced by Einstein will shortly necessitate a new type of *deterrence*: no longer military and nuclear, as it had to be when the major danger was the 'atomic bomb', but this time political and societal. Unless social disintegration has already entered an irreversible phase, with the decline in the nuclear family and the boom in the population unit of the **single-parent**.

ESCAPE VELOCITY

'The Earth is our mother, the Sky is our father.'

'Localization is pitiless,' the traveller Victor Segalen once remarked.[1] Pitiless, yes, like the here and now of a fact. But tomorrow, with the spread of long-distance interaction, it will become *pitiful*.

The resistance of distances having finally ceased, the world's expanse will lay down its arms, once known as duration, extension and horizon.

'The Earth teaches us a lot more about ourselves than all the books in the world, *because it resists us*. Man only finds himself when he measures himself against an obstacle,' noted the aviator Saint-Exupéry. The Earth, and the moon too, from the moment man set foot on it.

Gradually to break down all resistance, all dependence on the local, to wear down the opposition of duration and of extension, not only with regard to the terrestrial horizon but also to the circumterrestrial altitude of our natural satellite: the goal of science and technology has indeed now been attained. To eradicate the gap, to put an end to the scandal of the interval of space and time that used to separate man so unacceptably from his objective: all this is well on the way to being achieved. But at what cost? Surely at the cost of making pitiful, pitiful for all time, not only all those countries crossed in near total indifference, but the world, *the space-world*.

★

Conqueror of the length that drags, the passenger of the communications vehicle has eliminated one by one the obstacles that none the less allowed him to exist here and now in motion.[2] From that moment, he not only pollutes nature but also its grandeur, its life-size magnitude.

If the **object** is what is thrown in front of us – *ob-jactus* – then it is inseparable from the *traject* or *path* (journey) and its headlong rush, visual perspective being accompanied for the **subject** by a temporal perspective which our sciences, our technosciences of communication have not stopped shifting, endlessly speeding up the image at the risk of shortly sparking off an accident in this *traffic flow of the real* which all the signs already indicate will be unprecedented.

Since the philosophers of Antiquity, whom modern physicists have proved right, we have known from experience that *time is the form of matter in motion*.[3] But what seems to have been forgotten is that if time is not an 'independent incorporeal', it immediately introduces the necessity of a new figure for the accident: 'a particular accident of a number of states which are themselves accidents'.[4]

In other words, and still according to Epicurus, *time is the accident to end all accidents*, for we associate it with night and day and their component parts and similarly with feelings and their absence, motion and rest, deeming any accident in these to be called *Time*.[5]

To better size up the 'temporal catastrophe' which the events of this *fin de siècle* are not managing to cover up so very well at the moment, let us hear this time not from a great traveller or aviator, but from one of the astronauts involved in man's first steps on the moon, Buzz Aldrin: 'The Eagle has just landed, *the lunar module is perfectly still and that's a very weird sensation*. For me, a space flight is synonymous with movement. *But the module isn't moving, as though it were planted here from the beginning of time*.'[6]

It is indeed a matter of a 'beginning', the beginning not only of the conquest of the otherworld of extra-planetary space alone, but *another beginning of time*. This sudden immobility, this forced and paradoxical rest of non-motion in the space and time of another planet are literally without precedent: lunar time is no longer the same as the earth's; this time split, revealed to the astronauts by the very particular inertia of the night star, already offers them – and them alone – a glimpse of the interference of *lived time* with *astronomic time*, much more than with the *local time* of a lunar region so aptly named: *Tranquillity Base.*

Unable to get their bearings within the expanse of this *terra incognita*, the astronauts are not so much *on the moon* as in the gravitational inertia of a *fixed point*, without *spatial* reference and without *temporal* precedence, each one of them having tested for himself *de facto* **Zeno**'s paradox: *the paradox of the immobility of a path.*

Suddenly what is 'thrown in front of them' is an **object**; only, an object without parallel. Mankind's objective since the beginnings of astronomical observation is finally attained: the visual perspective of the Quattrocento, as well as that offered by Galileo's telescope, are outdistanced, outmoded by the incomparable emergence of a new *temporal perspective.*

Since the 'path' (improperly named the conquest of space) has finally freed itself from the reference axis of our native Earth, it ends up finding a completely separate space between the **subject** and the **object**, extra-worldly trajectivity slipping in beside ordinary subjectivity and objectivity.

And so the target attained by the arrow of the Apollo 11 mission is not so much Earth's satellite, 'the moon', as the pathway itself.

The being of the path of the movement involved in the conquest of space finally established its credentials in that very peculiar inertia of the Sea of Tranquillity.

But to better grasp the importance of this historic accident, of the telescoping achieved by man's moon landing, which extends to the otherworld Saint-Exupéry's claim that 'the Earth teaches us *a lot more* than all the books in the world', we need to go back three centuries, to the exact moment when geology discovered the *deep time* of the very density of our planet.

As Paolo Rossi so aptly puts it in his essay, *The Dark Abyss of Time,* 'Men in Hooke's times had a past of six thousand years; those of Kant's times were conscious of a past of millions of years.'[7]

This sudden overtaking of history, this plunge into the mists of time that happens at the end of the seventeenth century could in fact be compared with the leap into the dark of a sidereal expanse that was to culminate, at the end of this twentieth century, in the landing of man on the moon.

In that distant age, which corresponds more or less to the beginning of the 'Age of Enlightenment', the discovery of the immensity of time must certainly have seemed a truly major event, but I think it is going a bit far to say, as some do, that 'we cannot hope to match its import again', at the very moment when we are witnessing the liberation of time's arrow, the arrow of a universal time now experienced, lived, by 'extra-worldly' voyagers like Aldrin, Armstrong and a handful of others. But also, more especially, the emergence of a *global* time that may well dispense with the concrete importance of the *local* time of geography that once made history.[8]

But before we ask ourselves what is, and especially what will in the near future be, *the lack of depth of the present*, in an age of now universal communications, we should, I think, reconsider this gradual awareness of a geological layer *without memory*, as well as the breakdown, the telluric collapse, of knowledge of *the depth of the past*.

Towards the end of the seventeenth century, then, the idea arises, stemming from the new study of stratigraphy, that geology contains a hidden perspective and that this is to be found *everywhere beneath our feet* cropping up, erupting, here and there, through certain tectonic shifts, sometimes revealing above ground the mass of a time without memory. It is a safe bet that at the time this awareness, soon universally shared, must have considerably reinforced the very notion of a fundamental localization, the *hic et nunc* of a growing materialism.

To find yourselves gathered together, here and now, directly above a lithospheric mantle concealing millions of *matter-years* certainly did not do anything to diminish the value of 'nature' or of its grandeur, as would the later discovery of those billions of *light-years* that separate us, so they say, from the accident that gave birth to time.

'Exoticism is everything that is different,' according to Victor Segalen, that unrepentant traveller, who sized up every locality mercilessly.

I think we can say in this regard that the discovery of the **time-matter** that serves as a basis for the experience of motion and of being must, with the growth of self-awareness, have firmly grounded 'individualism', that fixed point of inertia that once justified every process of settling down; whereas, at the beginning of the twentieth century, *a contrario*, with Einstein, Hubble and Wegener, *the expansion of the Universe* and the sudden *continental drift* for their part highlighted the importance of exoticism, **time–light** making us suddenly forget both the extent and the mass of the time depth of our native habitat.

So we might note that if the emergence of the *deep time* of matter (geology) is fundamentally *endotic*, the *universal time* of light (cosmology) is *exotic*, inscribed in a dilatation phenomenon that endlessly renews our spatio-temporal references, since, as Stephen Hawking explains, 'In relativity, there were already several space-time curves.'

But in both these cases of historical awareness, what emerges, what crops up is no longer just a spatial and indeed *material* catastrophism, that of tellurism; it is a temporal and *immaterial* catastrophism, that of cosmic expansion.

Actually, if the **accident** is solely *what occurs* and not, like **substance**, *what is*, then the more the local time of history passes and fades, the more its accidental character is revealed, the past few centuries bringing 'to light' the phases of this temporal apocalypse whose probability Epicurus once pointed out to us.

The *cyclical* time of the world's origins and the *linear* time (the sagittal time of time's arrow) of a chronological history would then be superseded by a *spherical* time, the 'dromospherical' time of light (or of its cone, if you prefer) overtaking in the near future the old circle of bygone centuries.

Only, what this cleverly skirts round, thereby promoting some **global** time, is quite simply the **local** time of a history acted out on the surface of a planet within the very particular alternation of terrestrial night and day, under the influence of the specific gravity of one star among many.

After all the carrying on about the sudden depth of geological time beyond the depth of the Mosaic chronology of the Judaeo-Christian scriptures, how can we take this sudden amplification of time beyond the eternal return of the same without some reservations?

Already the two times of the 'line' and the 'cycle', by their very division, posed a certain number of particularly arduous stereoscopic questions for philosophy. But this new 'third dimension' of our old fourth dimension of time comes back down to asking ourselves *what is left* of nature as well as what remains of past magnitude.

Must we 'have pity on the world' from now on, as ecology suggests we should? Beg for mercy for its pathetic expanse?

If localization, restriction to a particular place, has suddenly become so pitiful for the immobile armchair navigator of this waning millennium, does this really mean we must now have pity on a *real space* that has already been discredited to the sole advantage of the *real time* of instantaneous exchanges or, on the contrary, hold our ground against such discrimination?

'All mortal greatness is but disease,' declared Herman Melville.[9] But when such greatness is no longer that of a proud sea captain but of a science without a conscience, *what disease are we talking about?*

What will be left tomorrow of the last 'surface records' of geography as we know it or of the second dimension of geometry if this new 'flood', the forecast temporal catastrophe, further intensifies the catastrophe in geological space?

After the *original accident* of continental immersion in that fluid mechanics, which not only the scriptures but also our own stratigraphy bear witness to, we can perhaps look forward to the *general accident* of an immersion of local space-time in the electromagnetic and wave mechanics of *time-light*, the waning importance of the time zones soon reproducing the disappearance of land above water level.

If this were in fact to happen, then the Earth, our *space-world*, would indeed be 'sick', struck down with a disease without any known precedent. And that would be a pity for the length, breadth and depth of a space rendered unreal by the artifice of a limit-speed that would effectively *wipe out* both history and the memory of it, since the well-known *desertification* of the geographical expanse would itself be outstripped by that of (chronogeographic) duration, *the desert of world time* – of a **global** time – complementing the desert of flora and fauna rightly decried by ecologists.

If we turn now to the sea or to the great deserts of infertility, what do we find? That there is no more surface, no more relief worthy of the name; just a *line*, a skyline. With the advent of world time, a parody of that of astronomy, the desert is getting bigger, *the perspective of local space is vanishing* and, with it, not only the apparent skyline, but also the whole panoply of surfaces recording movement.

The inertia of the fixed point then rounds off the loss of habitable surface areas, *the perspective of world time*, of the real time of immediacy, taking over both from that of the visible space of Quattrocento perspectivism and from that of the local time of the historic event occurring here and now.

This unprecedented accident, representing the end of the road for history, recalls the situation mentioned earlier of the astronaut on lunar soil: unsure where he is exactly, unsteady on his feet – like Aldrin in 1969 – he observes a barren horizon beneath a night sky which is no longer the skyline of a landscape, still less that of a country of some description, but merely *a site*, a situation, the touchdown point of the moon landing.

Besides, the very name 'Sea of Tranquillity' for a place devoid of any apparent dynamics illustrates the paradox of this sudden loss of 'surfaces' to the benefit of the 'point' that any extra-worldly voyage secretly entails. Strangely, another aspect of astronautics further reinforces the ambiguity of this temporal catastrophe that the very notion of 'conquest of space' today scarcely conceals. According to ancient Chinese wisdom, *you should never sacrifice mobility to safety*. But on the moon a while ago, as on the earth these days, this is what happens before our very eyes. Twenty-five years ago, the *emancipation of the journey* from terrestrial soil that drove the astronauts to land in the Sea of Tranquillity effectively required such a sacrifice to ensure the safety of the Apollo 11 mission.

It is understandable that the very notion of a *round trip* rather than just a 'one-way' catastrophe justified this elementary precaution. But, to make the point again: since it was no longer a question of extension but of duration, the question of the *irreversibility of sagittal time* once again came into its own; the arrow of time of the moon mission escaped not only gravitational references but also earth's spatio-temporal references, to wind up in the end registering only within the parameters of the laws of astronautics.

Einstein asserted that 'nothing in the Universe is fixed'. In the Sea of Tranquillity, the American astronauts' 'fixed point' is merely a *touchdown site* within the time of the trip from the earth to the moon. And the pitiless nature of this extraterrestrial pseudo-localization has less to do with some kind of **position** within a territorial unity easily travelled than with the astronauts' **situation** within the safe harbour of non-movement: *the inertia of a dead centre.*

Being not so much on the moon as outside the earth's field, Armstrong and Aldrin have to sacrifice their natural mobility to safety. With low reserves of energy, water and oxygen, their time is ticking away; and that time, that duration, is the time of a *countdown,* for their presence on the lunar landing site is only ever a precarious situation or, more accurately, an imprisoning one, forays outside the lunar module presenting the same pitfalls as the celebrated *extra-vehicular spacewalks* outside artificial satellites revolving in the interstellar void.

According to specialists in logistics – in other words, in the security of supplies – '*the more movement increases, the more control increases*', finally extending to the most intimate conditions of personal survival.

So what extends, spreads out, is not so much 'place', the extension of the real space of one planet among others; it is the extent of control, of an 'environmental control' that takes over from the continental surface area, from the three dimensions of a habitable space for the being endowed with movement.

Aqualung, DataSuit, pressurized cockpit or space shuttle: the situation is now much the same everywhere. Here, in the Sea of Tranquillity or down there, over the hill of the moon's horizon, on that Earth of living beings who, for a time, experience freedom of movement.

When control tends systematically to replace the environment, its height, breadth and depth, the prediction of the navigator Herman Melville effectively comes true: '*All mortal greatness is but disease.*' And this disease, this passing incapacity, has a name: *paralysis.* Paralysis of a world, of a 'space-world' that has abandoned itself to the time of the finite world.

In this paradoxical situation, what is 'incapable' or, at any rate, *incapacitated*, is the environment and its properties. The immensity of the cosmic void or of deep time are merely handicaps for the atrophied being whose safety now takes precedence over all activity, to the point where, for him, the concrete environment has only a single dimension left, **the point**. The point, plus time; only, an astronomic and universal time. Encapsulated in the arrow of cosmic time, cut off from local time by his very travels, the extra-worldly navigator (or the worldly televiewer) is the victim of an unprecedented inertia, for this inertia suddenly gets tangled up with the pre-eminence of time over real space, interactivity taking the place of traditional mobilizing activity.

In a text illustrating the vanity of a technology whose power would soon lead Europe to chaos, Martin Heidegger paraphrased Melville: 'All greatness lies in the assault.'

Once the Second World War was over, though, Heidegger specified that: 'This is not just an assault mounted against something remaining. War is what initially opens up and develops the unheard of, till then never before said or thought. When war is over, what was does not disappear, but the world turns away.'

Turned away, skirted round by satellites doing the rounds, like some useless thing in the way, the world stops resisting and caves in completely in the face of the assault on what remains. Just a bit further down the track and whether Saint-Exupéry likes it or not: *the Earth will no longer teach us a thing*.

The resistance of distances having ceased, the lost world will send us back to our solitude, a multiple solitude of some billions of individuals whom the multimedia are preparing to organize in quasi-cybernetic fashion. After two world wars *in space* that ended in the gradual loss of the *space-world*, with the conquest of the air and of circumterrestrial space, the world war *in time* will lead, for its part, to the loss of our freedom of movement: an irremediable but discreet loss, in which *everything will remain as it was*, except for being qualitatively discredited in this time-world that will respond in future to our every desire.

Then, alongside the *deep time* of geology and of history, the *superficial time* of remote interaction will rise up and take over from the surface areas of a vanished expanse. The real time of transmission, once and for all outstripping the real space of transport, will fulfil the prophecy of Saint Jerome when he said: '*The world is already full and no longer holds us.*'

For a quarter of a century 'trajectography' – tracking – has effectively replaced 'geography'.

From now on there is a path independent of *any locality* and especially of any *localization*.

A path inscribed solely in time, in an astronomic time that is gradually contaminating all the various local times. It is true that the science of the flight of a projectile, the ballistics of a cannonball, a shell or missile, already anticipated this event, but did so using a *gravitational localization* linked to the centre of the Earth. With an extra-planetary outlet, this 'reference axis' in turn disappears. From the exocentration of a body in flight above the ground we suddenly swap to egocentration: the centre is no longer located outside; it is its own reference, its 'driving-axis'. The inertial centre serves as the world's axis, but of a small inner world which turns protruded man into *a planet,* though a living planet, launched into the void of a cosmic time and not, as often claimed, into the space-time of the intersidereal universe.

What spatiality are we talking about, anyway, once we have lost all support, all lift and, therefore, all postural reference?

If it is true that the question of 'spatiality' is never to be confused with the need for the meteorological atmosphere of a habitable space, it is none the less always conditioned by the nature of our *position* in the movement of displacement and in its *orientation*, since velocity does not exist without the vector of *direction*.

Now, what 'spatiality' could we possibly mean when the only thing that remains is the *being of the path*, of a pathway wholly identified with the 'subject' and the 'object' in motion, with no other reference beyond itself?

This comes down to the whole philosophical issue of a being which is less *in the world* than *out of it*, this 'out-of-this-world' being going out of its way, though, to pretend to inhabit the real world.

Having got this far, a certain question makes itself felt. But it is a question that has no answer; an almost insane and definitely disturbing question that defies science and philosophy: 'If there is no void without the full, or light without darkness, can we not, should we not, ask ourselves whether space is conceivable without matter and without surface?'

In an age when the interface of the instantaneous transmission of interaction is gearing up to dominate the time-honoured *surface of inscription of action*, surely it would be appropriate to question the very concepts of space and void, as the limit-speed of electromagnetic radiation gears up to remodel the human environment along cybernetic lines.

If time is *what happens without us* and if, again according to Epicurus, that time gets confused with 'the accident to end all accidents' of a process of transmission that is currently spreading, then surely we are forced to re-examine not only the classic notion of **materiality**, but also those of **spatiality** and **temporality**, this 'space-time-matter' which modern physicists have done their best not only to rope together in relativistic fashion but also to fuse, indeed, to confuse?

If this is indeed the case, then we need also to reconsider the whole notion of **accident**, of a 'transfer accident' that now conditions our apprehension of reality.

★

Let us now consider the 'out-of-this-world' aspect of the extra-planetary emancipation achieved by the lunar mission and, more recently, by the revelation of a virtual space or **cyberspace**. In both cases, we are forced to meet the same challenge, the challenge of a sudden 'loss of reality' of space-time-matter. Here, the accident is no longer a *local* accident, precisely situated in the space of an action and in the *presence of a being, there, here and now*, but a *general* accident which globally undermines all 'presence' and promotes a 'telepresence' without consistency and, more particularly, without a true spatial position, since the remote interaction of a being at once absent and acting (teleacting) redefines the very notion of *being there*.

At the heart of this virtual space, where media control (feedback) conditions and takes over from the real space of the immediate environment, **cyberspace** looms up like a *transfer accident* in substantial reality. Suddenly, what gets accidentally damaged is no longer the substance, the materiality of the tangible world, it is the whole of its constitution.

Just as the astronaut broke free of the reality of his native world in landing on the moon, the cybernaut momentarily leaves the reality of mundane space-time and inserts himself into the *cybernetic strait-jacket* of the virtual-reality environment control programme.

In either case, however, the crisis is clear, as much for the 'object' as for the 'subject': the only thing emancipated in the end is the journey, a 'path', the tracking of which is rigorously controlled by the instantaneous speed of emission and reception of information provided by a computer that has suddenly become *the arranger of tangible reality*.

So, it is clear that it is indeed the implementation of the limit-speed of electromagnetic waves that today *brings to light* the virtual reality of cybernetics, the realism of which is gearing up to replenish the realism of the mass and extension of the real space of our immediate environment – that none the less privileged place of all action worthy of the name.

We can now understand the overwhelming necessity of identifying a *third* and final 'interval' of the *light* type, alongside the classic intervals of the *space* and *time* types.

In the age of the industrial revolution in transport, when geography still bore the brunt of most travel, the gradual acceleration of *relative* speeds did not escape the classic conditions of 'position' and 'localization' and, in particular, of the (vectorial) 'direction' of the travelling object. By contrast, with the recent 'informational' revolution in transmission, the absolute speed of remote interaction requires a trajectography independent of the reference axis of earth's gravity, in order to be able to privilege management of the never-ending feedback of information instantaneously emitted and received.

Whence the emergence of a *paradoxical interval* of the 'light' type (the speed of light), both to evaluate the two-way path of wave packets and, especially, to relativize the intervals of space and duration that once, however, went with history and geography.

So, at the end of this century, the *general accident* arises from the urgent necessity of a *neutral-sign* interval to compensate for the notoriously inadequate measurement provided by the traditional intervals of *positive sign* (time) and *negative sign* (space). A 'fractal' interval of the light type that suddenly comes along and overturns the binomial measurement of duration and extension alike.

Already fundamentally depreciated through the material pollution of substances (atmosphere, hydrosphere, lithosphere), our planet is more subtly depreciated by the *immaterial pollution* of distances (dromospherical), which leads us to free ourselves from the 'solid ground' of the tangible experience of geography – thanks, notably, to the acquisition of speeds known as 'orbital' or 'escape' velocity, but which also force us to lose our bearings, to lose touch with the surfaces of matter just so we can inscribe our 'interactive' action in the off-field of a gravitationless space, just so we can teleact instantaneously in the *cybernetic trajectory* of a second reality; the very notions of relief or of volume no longer solely affecting matter and its 'third dimension', but *the very reality of the fourth dimension*, thereby provoking this 'temporal catastrophe' – this real-time accident – that now doubles the ancient 'material catastrophe' of which the deep time of 'geology' still bears the scars.

So, along with the permanent dilation of a time that is now not so much cyclical as *spherical* (dromospherical), the depth of the past is not the only depth that is getting bigger. For we are now seeing the amplification of the *present*; only, of a *present continued, inflated*, that is nothing more than the *superficial time* of a telepresence that now reproduces for us the surprise, in short the utter amazement of eighteenth-century folk confronted by the 'geological' discovery of a *deep time* going back several million years.

And it is curious to note that this 'topological' shift in the nature of time, which the theory of relativity does, however, imply, did not disturb the historians but only the physicists, the astrophysicists, such as Stephen Hawking and a few other contemporaries of the discovery of the expansion of the universe.

Yet, this sudden leap from the cyclical time of the eternal return of the same to the cosmic expansion of a *spherical time* – or, more precisely, space-time – ought to have excited philosophers and not just men of science. Unless, of course, as disciples of 'historical materialism', both camps let themselves be hoodwinked by the dominant ideology of *a one-dimensional duration*, the line of that sagittal time of an arrow that never reaches its target. If we leave out the hidden face of temporality by which I mean its absence, *eternity*, the 'eternity' which, Rimbaud tells us, a being cannot fail *to regain*.

But let us get back to this temporal dilation, the welling up of a duration that determines not only the astronomic retreat of the past and the probable extension of the future, but also, for us earthlings, the sudden globalization of the present, a new flood of 'real time' now washing over the earth more thoroughly than water fills the seas.

Where *local* time was able to 'make history', based on geography, *world* time effectively abolishes it, at least in its actual localization, since the **space–world** gives way to time, but to the **time–world** of an instantaneous trajectography bearing no reference to the ground or to the surface, the *interface* of emission and instantaneous reception now supplanting the whole of the surface areas constitutive of material space. Few theorists, I believe, have really tackled this rapid displacement (this journey) in the notions of space and time due to Einstein's relativity. More importantly, few have picked up the attendant migration in the notions of 'mass', 'duration' and 'extension' that the sudden *globalized expansion of the present* represents for us.[10]

Indeed, wherever interactive telecommunication requires a space free of obstacles and thus free of resistance to the accelerated propulsion of information, a sort of *superconductive medium* necessarily pops up that will do away with any kind of telluric 'landmark' as well as any geophysical 'surface record', since the screen itself is already fading and will soon disappear, paving the way for series transmissions broadcast simultaneously into a **DataSuit** and into a stereoscopic vision helmet that transmutes the receiver into a **human terminal** – as though the ultimate surface or, rather, the ultimate interface were the *occipital cortex*!

It is easy to see now how the erasure of political boundaries in Europe and the world is just the tip of the iceberg, the harbinger of a temporal catastrophe in which what sinks and disappears without a trace is not just the *resistance of distances*, but the resistance of the *dimensions* of material space – the point, the line, the surface or volume gradually losing their classic geometric attributes as this **superconductive medium** alluded to above suddenly proliferates madly. An immaterial medium whose fluid mechanics has little to do

with water or air and much to do with the waves that carry information.

So, before our very eyes – and I use the phrase advisedly since
physical optics wins out over geometric optics here – the notions of
centre and periphery are suddenly redefined. These now have less to
do with the 'space' of surfaces and volumes than with 'time', the
time of that inflated present known as *real time* which today governs
man's activities on a worldwide scale.

At the end of the millennium, the *centre of real time* supersedes the
centre of real space in historical and political importance. Wherever the
nodal of interactive telecommunications prevails over the **central** of
active communication, the *intensive* definitively towers over the *extensive*.

With the sudden but subtle 'inflation of the present', of a present
globalized by teletechnologies, present time occupies centre stage not
only of history (between past and future), but especially of the geography of the **globe**. So much so that a new term has recently been
coined, **glocalization**, to designate the very latest centrality of real
time that is nothing more than this 'superconductive medium' offering no resistance to the electrodynamics of telematic impulses and
whose *drag coefficient is zero* since it is itself only the spectacular
manifestation of the properties of this third and final *interval of neutral
sign* physicists are now talking about![11]

The **present**, thereby inflated to world-space scale, to the point
where it outdoes diurnal–nocturnal alternation as the usual measure
of *local* time, is thus indeed that of 'light' or, more precisely, of that
time-light that now forces itself on the **time–matter** of surface
areas, masses and places.

But in the face of this worldwide deployment of present time, an
often hidden dimension of Einstein's theory of relativity suddenly
springs to mind: that of the **eternal present**. Curiously, this
unavoidable notion has been forgotten, or more likely dropped, even

though it largely clarifies the scientist's refusal to accept, along with Edwin Hubble and a few others, the principle of universal expansion. In fact, if anyone is not a 'creationist', or an advocate of a 'stationary' universe, it has to be Einstein, the very person who declared that: *nothing in the universe is fixed*! He of all people can hardly be accused of intellectual conservatism!

So why has Einstein's rejection of the 'inflationary universe' phenomenon arising from the **big bang** been so woefully misinterpreted in endlessly reopened postmortem proceedings based on assumptions rather than facts?

For Einstein, the present is already 'the centre of time'; the past of the original **big bang** is not, and scientifically cannot be, that *old* centre. The true centre is always *new*, the centre is perpetual, or to put it even more precisely, the 'present' is an **eternal present**.

For the three tenses of (chronological) succession – past, present and future – Einstein substituted a (chronoscopic or dromoscopic) *exposure time*: underexposed, exposed, overexposed.

In Einstein's view, time's arrow is an arrow of light and cannot be the magic arrow of the cosmic archer. Hence, his approach to 'kinematic optics' and his anticipation of the famous gravitational mirages and other astrophysical aberrations which organize not only vision for the human observer, but, more especially, the scientific interpretation of phenomena, based on the absolute limit-speed of both light and universal gravity – that is to say, 300,000 kilometres per second.

The centre of time would thus be **light** or, more exactly, the speed of information-carrying waves.

It is no longer, then, a matter of counting the years or the centuries, on the basis of the traditionalist alternation of night and day; it is now a matter of basing 'the science of time' on the speed barrier, that **time-light barrier** that organizes both the 'extension' and the 'duration' of the phenomenal ageing processes of **time-matter**.

Since this finite yet absolute speed is not a phenomenon but the relationship between phenomena, the **spatiotemporal continuum** cannot have a 'centre' – still less an origin – beyond this very relativity or, in other words, beyond the 'time-light' of an exposure time that imposes itself on the historic and classic time of succession.

'*Give me your intuition of the present and I'll give you the past and the future,*' Emerson, the founder of transcendentalism, used to say.

Chronometer or speedometer? How can we not contest the linear and unfolding nature of time today? Of this time that passes, this course of *chronos* that reproduces the course of the sun and which clockfaces do not so much logically demonstrate as mechanically '*monstrate*'.

For some, the only suffering is that caused by the passing days. Let them rest assured: *tomorrow the present will no longer pass* or, at least, hardly.

Inflated to fill the dimensions of the world's space, the time of the present world flashes us a glimpse on our screens of another regime of temporality that reproduces neither the chronographic succession of the hands of our watches nor the chronological succession of history.

Outrageously puffed up by all the commotion of our communication technologies, the *perpetual present* suddenly serves to illuminate duration. Reproducing the alternation between night and the solar day that once organized our ephemerides, the *endless day* of the reception of events produces an instantaneous lighting of reality that leaves the customary importance of the successive nature of facts in the shade; factual sequences little by little losing all mnemonic value and so boosting the dazzlement of this *hypercentre of time* that the live emission and reception of information represents so perfectly.

In his memoirs of the first moon landing, Buzz Aldrin in his own way confirms this disqualification of sunlight. Listen to what he has to say from the surface of the night star: 'The light is also weird. Since there's no atmosphere, the phenomenon of refraction disappears, so much so that you go directly from total shadow into sunlight, without any transition. *When I hold my hand out to stick it in the light, you'd think I was crossing the barrier to another dimension.*' It is as though, for the astronaut, shadow and light were two new dimensions, inasmuch as any kind of transition no longer exists for him, the loss of the phenomena of atmospheric refraction producing a different perception of reality.

For the rest of us, inhabitants of Mother Earth, the same 'loss of transition' is occurring at this *fin de siècle*, and the sudden diminished importance of the refraction of sunlight provides grounds for calling into question the different degrees of illumination which, before the invention of electricity, still marked the hours of the day or the days of the year.

Under the indirect light from screens and other control centres of the optoelectronic transmission of events, the *time of chronological succession* evaporates, paving the way for an *instantaneous and chronoscopic exposure time* as harsh as that floodlighting of which Aldrin tells us: 'On the moon, the sun shines on us like a giant spotlight.'

Even if we are still talking about the same 'sun', we are no longer talking about the same 'light' or, consequently, the same 'time'. *Earth time*, the time of its matter, is not in fact the *time-light* that shines on the men of the lunar mission. For atmospheric transition has disappeared and, with it, the fade-in/fade-out of that optical refraction due to the thin gaseous film that allows us not only to breathe – and so to live – but also *to count time*, thanks to the transitive nature of days, hours and minutes, the sequential unfolding of our earthly sojourn being only ever an 'artefact', *a film of the sky* and its meteorology.

Willing victims of the 'total performance syndrome', another form of 'delusions of grandeur', our astronauts were thus the first to glimpse this **general accident** that awaits us tomorrow, down here, in this *already-here tomorrow* of the perpetual present of real-time technologies.

Neil Armstrong, for instance, only became aware of what he had done 'up there' once he had come back down to earth. *In reality, he did not really live it; he just carried it out.*

And for eight long years, from 1971 to 1979, our extraterrestrial astronaut was to take refuge with his family on a farm in his native Ohio. For his part, Mike Collins, the third man of the Apollo 11 mission, had the strange feeling *of having been both present and absent at the same time, on earth as on the moon,* testing out for us the loss of the **hic et nunc**, that total and fortunately momentary loss of the positional referent.

As for Aldrin, after two nervous breakdowns, several detoxification treatments for alcohol abuse and a divorce, he was to wind up in a psychiatric ward. As though the two most famous crews in contemporary history – that of the Enola Gay, which dropped the atomic bomb, and that of the Apollo 11 space capsule – had been the prophets of doom of humanity's unhappy future.

Let us hear what the late, lamented Jacques Ellul had to say about this at once physical and metaphysical relationship between 'light' and 'duration': 'When Genesis tells us that the first creation is light, surely this is to tell us precisely that it is "the creation of time", since light and time are indissoluble.'[12] Ellul goes on to say: 'Arising from truth, *light literally gives rise to reality*; for, again in the text of Genesis, light is *the appearance of time.*'

To tamper with light, with the illumination of the world, is thus to attack *reality*. Illumination's lack of place gives place to time, to that tangible duration without which no reality of events can exist.

As for *truth*, that is quite a different thing from the much-vaunted effectiveness of the sciences and technologies of information. Hence the perceptual disorders and pathological behaviour of the astronauts after their emancipation; but equally, today, those experienced by our contemporaries, subject, in spite of themselves, to the hegemony of experts which Jacques Ellul further claims is the major temptation of our civilization: 'the bid to confuse **reality** and **truth** that consists in making it seem that the **real** and the **true** *coincide in a single and unique truth*.'[13]

Now, when this confusion goes beyond language, beyond this or that speculative practice, and also attacks the key notions of 'temporality' and 'spatiality', the confusion reaches Tower of Babel proportions; the great danger then is *disorientation* – spatial, certainly, but especially temporal disorientation.

Vertigo of a present-past or of a future that is already here, already seen, already given; a situation not so much **utopic** as **teletopical** which greatly affects being in the world, along with the very notion of a habitat.

When Neil Armstrong, for instance, thinks he has *performed* a task, but has never really *lived* it, or when Mike Collins has the strange sensation of being *doubly absent*, they are both signalling this fatal confusion that fragments the subject's personality. Such confusion is characteristic of the dreamlike states of drunkenness or the momentary hallucinations of narcosis, but especially of precocious senility.

Can we say, then, that this sudden splitting off from concrete reality on the part of our extraterrestrial voyagers is the product of the length of space travelled in their race towards the night star; or that it was the length of time of the lunar mission that produced this narcosis from out of the cosmic depths? No to both the above, and we would all agree, I am sure, that the long-haul navigation of, say, Magellan outdid by a long shot this little escapade, this weekend on the moon.

No, *the vertigo comes exclusively from extra-planetary emancipation,* from loss of the *sui generis* referents of the space-time so peculiar to the Earth. In other words, loss of Earth's 'light', the **light-matter** that involves both the time and the space of this 'planetary habitat' whose gravity has shaped even our physiology.

So we can see why today, if the idea of *information* tends to dominate the classic notions of *mass* and *energy*, this is only because it refers to the notion of absolute speed or, more specifically, to *the concept of the limit-speed of light*. Now would be the time to go back over the definition of this **time-light** that informs us of all spatial or temporal 'depth'.

Indeed, if light-matter is an appropriate form for occupying space made perceptible by the particular light of 'earth-matter', *time-light* is the prevalent form for occupying time, made tangible by the speed of light *in a vacuum*, the differentials of acceleration being easily explained by variations in the density of matter distributed throughout the universe.

So, if the space and time of matter combine to form the relativity continuum, we might add that these same notions are equally commingled in the *time of information* – indeed in the very notion of real time. And so we have then to conclude that the time of light and the space of matter (its density) constitute an inverse correlation, in which a reduction in material density translates as an acceleration in the said 'information', while any increase in this same density corresponds to its deceleration. This holds, even for the supremely hard-hardwearing diamond in the mineral realm.

This is how Louis de Broglie, who wrote *Matter and Light*, unveils for us his vision of the world: 'We might suppose that at the beginning of time, immediately following some divine **fiat lux**, light, at first alone in the world, little by little, by slow condensation, engendered the material universe such as we are able to contemplate it today, thanks to light.'[14]

Curiously, though, in this perfectly anthropic evocation of the 'great condenser', the word 'light' is ultimately equivalent to cosmic illumination, though de Broglie knows better than most that such **light** is the light of its **speed** and thus the light of the 'dromospheric' condensation of **space–time–matter**.

Time, then, never lets itself be seen outside the ageing of the structures of matter, but the speed of time-light, on the other hand, lets us see, perceive, not only the Earth, but also this 'universe' which no more surrounds us than space contains us, fashioned as we are by the sudden acceleration of a universal gravitation that is exactly equal to the acceleration of light in a vacuum.

'An hour is a lake. A day a sea, night an eternity,' Joseph Roth bitterly observed in 1938, on the eve of a world war. How can we fail to discover after him the inertia of a 'present' time that gets confused with the very fixity of places?

If *relative* speed means man's old age, the accelerated ageing of our cells, for man *absolute* speed means this disease which makes the newborn prematurely senile and which goes by the name of **progeria**.[15]

When the real instant prevails in intensity over the density of the extension of real space, *all duration freezes* and inertia reaches gigantic proportions.

Suddenly, immobility no longer has anything to do with the immobility of water on the surface of a lake, or that of the deep time of minerals. It is now *the immobility of all possible journeys or paths*. The time-light barrier then blocks off – along with the horizon of appearances – the horizon of action, the very reality of a space where all succession dissolves, where it is as though hours and days *had ceased to flow, surfaces ceased to extend*: what cropped up yesterday, here or there, now happens everywhere at once. The accident to end all accidents spreads in a flash and the centre of time – the endless present – leaves behind the centre of fixed space for good. There is no longer any 'here', everything is 'now'. The hypercentre of the intensive time of production of the real wins out once and for all over the former centrality of the extensive space of territories.

From that moment: '*the sum total of light is the world*'.[16]

Now let us take a look at what may well shortly become a sedentariness no longer confined to the local space of a suburb or a city or a region, but to the time of an endless perpetuation of the present: *contemporary man no longer arrives at, achieves, anything.* This is the total performance syndrome, already at work, as we saw, in our astronauts on their return from their extraterrestrial cruise.

If the here of incarceration has ceased to exist in the escape velocity of action at a distance – teleaction – its **now** none the less remains, an all-powerful and all-seeing now whose *pitiless* nature is incommensurable with the nature of the age-old localization of the **hic et nunc**. The split between **place** and **hour** has now been consummated.

The generalized arrival of transmission has taken over from the restricted arrival of transport. In days gone by, Joshua, the man of God, *stopped the sun*; today the man of science *stops the Earth*! A 'freeze frame' whereby the interactive experience of generalized teleaction will soon prolong the life sentence of the expanse of the space-world, to the exclusive advantage of the time-world of the real instant.

As Joseph Roth, whose sense of headlong flight is not unlike Kafka's sense of inertia, warned us: 'The world worth living in was doomed. The world that would follow it deserved no decent inhabitants.'[17]

No, what will remain inhabitable, in spite of everything, is the 'town', a town that is not now the City of the original urbanization of the real space of the continents, but the 'city to end all cities' of a world that will have become fundamentally transpolitical and in which synoecism will no longer mean, as it did in ancient Greece, the gathering of several villages into a single cosmopolitan **city-state**, but the joining or, rather, the telescoping of all cities into a single and unique **capital**, not so much metropolitan as **omnipolitan**. Solitary triumph of a sedentariness without a home front and without a hinterland, where information will dominate mass and expanse equally; the hypercentre of present time in turn becoming the sole reference axis of worldwide activity. An **axis mundi** likely to erase for ever all other forms of 'centralization', not merely urban but, indeed, human as well: 'the individual of the scientific age is losing his capacity to experience himself as a centre of energy'.[18]

As I said, a new word has recently appeared, to name the apparent paradox of a mix between the local time of an activity still precisely situated and the global time of generalized interactivity. That word is **glocalization** and, as we may well imagine, it applies not so much to 'multinationals' which are capable of managing their affairs in the two, equally globalized, dimensions of production and distribution, as to this virtual **world-city** that already contains within itself both the 'geographical' centre of the set of real agglomerations it brings together and the 'temporal' hypercentre of telecommunications that enable it to exist remotely. This it does, *by making itself present* to the other cities, thanks notably to the feats of the *time-sharing* that today supersedes the geopolitical sharing-out of territorial space, since from now on every *real* city is only ever the remote periphery, the great urban wasteland of this *virtual* city that rules over it totally or, better still, 'glocally'.

Directly involved in this **telecontinent** that is spreading over the expanse of **continents** now as discredited as the borders between nations, the **teletopic megacity** is the culmination of that 'cohabitation' initiated by the invention of Athens. But with one difference, since it is no longer a matter of the flourishing of a kind of **synoecism** in geographical space, the fruit of a spatial approach to politics, **isonomy**, the city centre signifying the city's autonomy, but a matter of a temporal and transpolitical perception: **isochrony**, whereby the centre of real time plays the role once allotted to the centre of real space in the Greek polis: that **kratos** which symbolically reproduced the axis of the world, the world of Mother Earth (*gaia*), whose autonomy and stability were assured only by its geocentric position at the heart of a cosmos where vertical and aerial liberation was both technically impossible and barred, if we confine ourselves to the Hebrew register this time, to catch a glimpse of *the shadow of the Tower of Babel*.

NOTES

Introduction (pp.1–6)

1 See the theory published jointly in 1991 by Professor R.J. Taylor of Sussex University and Professor Alexander Abian of the Mathematics Department of Iowa University.

2 G. Cohen-Tannoudji and M. Spiro, *La Matière-espace-temps*, Paris 1986.

3 *Les Chemins de la science* (a text based on the findings of a general report compiled by the Centre national de la recherche scientifique), Paris 1992, p. 9.

The Third Interval (pp.9–21)

1 G. Cohen Tannoudji and M. Spiro, *La Matière-espace-temps*.

2 Nicholas of Cusa (Nicolas Cusanos), *Of Learned Ignorance*, trans. Father Germain Heron, New Haven 1954, pp. 78–9. See also Giuseppe Bufo, *Nicolas de Cues*, Paris 1964.

3 Paul Virilio, *L'Inertie polaire*, Paris 1990.

The Perspective of Real Time (pp.22–34)

1 Edmund Husserl, *La Terre ne se meut pas*, Paris 1989.

2 Paul Virilio, *L'Espace critique*, Paris 1984.

3 Giulio Carlo Argan and Rolf Wittkower, *Perspective et histoire au Quattrocento*, Paris 1990.

4 Auguste Rodin, *L'Art: Entretiens réunis par P. Gsell*, Paris 1911, translated as Rodin, *Art – Conversations with Paul Gsell*, trans. Jacques de Caso and Patricia B. Sanders, Berkeley 1984, p. 32.

5 Maurice Merleau-Ponty, *Phenomenology of Perception*, trans. Colin Smith, London 1974, p. 203.

6 M. Dufourneaux, *L'Attrait du vide*, Paris 1967.

7 Parachutists who are free fall specialists often carry a small bag of talc or a rocket to mark the fall line for spectators on the ground, just before they open their parachutes.

The Law of Proximity (pp. 49–57)

1 Jean-Luc Marion, *L'Idole et la distance*, Paris, p. 206.

2 *D'Architectures*, No. 17, August 1991.

3 The notion of 'real time' corresponding to the primacy of the speed of light, a limit, and yet *finite*, speed that has constituted one of the constants of cosmology ever since Einstein.

Grey Ecology (pp. 58–68)

1 Jérôme Cardan, *Ma Vie*, Paris 1992.

2 Jacques-Yves Le Toumelin.

3 Karl Kraus, *Beim Wort Genommen*, Munich 1965. Originally published by Herbst in 1918.

4 G. d'Aboville, *Seul*, Paris 1992.

5 Kafka, *Letters to Milena*, trans. Tania and James Stern, London 1983, p. 183.

6 The Dromesko Aviary.

7 M. Scott Carpenter et al., *We Seven, by the Astronauts Themselves*, New York 1962.

Continental Drift (pp. 69–86)

1 Epicurus (341–270 BC).

2 The average wage of a worker in Portugal at the time was only 1,700 French francs, compared to a high of 7,000 francs in France.

3 The expression 'omnipolitan' is Marco Bertozzi's.

4 Note here the success in the (1994) Italian elections of 'Forza Italia', the party run by media mogul Silvio Berlusconi.

5 Taken from the study by Janet Abrams, *Lieux de travail mobile*.

6 Ibid.

7 The expression 'information shock' was coined by Emmanuel Monod, an engineer with IBM.

Eye Lust (pp. 89–102)

1 *L'Equilibre en pesanteur et en apesanteur*, Paris 1987.
2 *Les métaphores du virtuel*, IMAGINA 92.
3 IMAGINA 92.
4 Paul Virilio, 'L'Opération de la cataracte', in *Les Cahiers du Cinéma*, August 1986.
5 Henri IV, *Correspondance*.
6 DGC/DRET Document, June 1992.
7 *La Recherche*, February 1991.
8 *La Recherche*, September 1992.
9 'Le Cerveau en temps réel', in *La Recherche*, September 1992.

From Sexual Perversion to Sexual Diversion (pp. 103–18)

1 'I like having the kids, but I don't want them on my hands', an ad for the *Nouvelles frontières* travel agency chain.
2 In ancient China, being carted off in the bridal wagon was an essential part of the wedding ceremony.
3 Dan. Urry, 'Les Machines à protéine', in *Pour la Science*, February 1995.
4 Paul Virilio, 'La Conduite intérieure', in *L'Horizon négatif*, Paris 1984.
5 Saint-Pol Roux, *Vitesse*, Paris 1973.
6 Schopenhauer, 'On the Suffering of the World', in *Essays and Aphorisms*, trans. R.J. Hollingdale, London 1970, pp. 47–8.
7 Schopenhauer, 'On the Suffering of the World' (untranslated parts of chapter 7 of *Parerga und Paralipomena*, Munich 1913).
8 Ibid.
9 Ibid.
10 Ibid.
11 'En attendant', in *Lettre d'information de la Maison de toutes les chimères*, No. 3, December 1994.
12 Saint-Pol Roux, *Cinéma vivant*, Paris 1972.
13 *Le Monde*, 23 February 1994.
14 P. Georges, 'Le Cybersexe à l'index', in *Le Monde*, 15 March 1995.

Escape Velocity (pp. 119–45)

1 Victor Segalen, *Equipée*, Paris 1983, p. 112.

2 Ibid. p. 57.

3 Epicurus.

4 Epicurus.

5 *Accidens*: that which occurs.

6 Buzz Aldrin and Malcolm McDonnell, *Men from Earth*, New York 1989.

7 Paolo Rossi, *The Dark Abyss of Time*, Chicago 1984, p. ix; quoted in Stephen Jay Gould, *Time's Arrow, Time's Cycle*, London 1991, p. 3.

8 Stephen Jay Gould, *Time's Arrow*, p. 17. Gould says: 'the discovery of time was so central, so sweet, and so provocative, that we cannot hope to match its import again'.

9 Herman Melville, *Moby Dick*, Oxford 1988, p. 76. The full sentence is: 'Be sure of this, O young ambition, all mortal greatness is but disease.'

10 In the past, when *local* time dominated history, the notion of *surface* seemed adequate. Today, in the age of *global* time, the notion of *interface* reigns supreme.

11 *Glocalisation* is an English-language term referring to the fact that from now on the *local* is inseparable from the *global*.

12 Jacques Ellul, *La Parole humiliée*.

13 Ibid.

14 Louis de Broglie, *Physique et microphysique*, Paris 1947, translated as *Physics and Microphysics*, trans. Martin Davidson, London 1955, p. 69 (translation here modified).

15 *Progeria* is precocious senility and it currently affects one child in 250,000.

16 Jacques Roubaud.

17 Joseph Roth, *The Radetzky March*, trans. Joachim Neugroschel, London 1995, p. 188.

18 Paul Valéry.

GLOSSARY

baryons elementary particles (hadrons) composed of three quarks; can undergo strong interactions

BASE jump a parachute jump from a fixed point (especially a high building or promontory) rather than an aircraft; BASE is an acronym for building, antenna-tower, span, earth – the types of structure used

brown dwarf a celestial body of intermediate size between a giant planet and a small star, believed to emit mainly infrared radiation

cadastral of, or showing the extent, value and ownership of, land, especially for taxation

chorography the systematic description of regions or districts

closed-loop system this refers to any device or machine that regulates itself in some way, thanks to the incorporation of feedback from the output into the input; a sensor at the output end generates a signal that is sent back to the input to regulate the machine's behaviour

collimate make (telescopes or rays) accurately parallel

diastase medical term denoting the process whereby an enzyme converts starch and glycogen into simple sugars

excimer a dimer existing only in an excited state, used in some lasers (excited + dimer, dimer being a compound consisting of two identical molecules linked together)

eyeballing a parachuting term referring to assessment of height during free fall to determine the moment the parachute should be opened; this assessment can be made with one's eyes, without reference to the altimeter normally used by parachutists; opening height is normally 2,000 feet or

600 metres; 'ground rush', the sensation of the ground rushing up at the parachutist, only occurs below this level

force-feedback technology for remote-control operation of a robot using feedback that gives the operator a sense of being where the robot is

Géode the spherical cinema building opened in 1984 in the Cité des Sciences at the Parc de la Villette on the outskirts of Paris

keyboarding data collection by means of computer

loop a repeating sequence of operations in a computer programme, repeated a controlled number of times until or while a particular condition is satisfied; a management system in which the terminals are arranged in a line, the ends of which loop round to join the central unit; in electricity, a complete circuit of a current

nano- denoting a factor of ten

oculometer eye tracking device

optoelectronics the branch of technology involving the convergence of optical and electronic technology and concerned with the generation, processing and detection of optical signals that represent electrical quantities; major areas of application include communications and computing

photonics produced by or involving the flow of photons, a photon being a quantum of electromagnetic radiation energy (by analogy with electronics)

Planck's length the length $(Gh/2\pi c^3)^{1/2}$, where G is the gravitational constant, h is Planck's constant and c the speed of light

pyknoleptic from pyknolepsy, a medical term denoting childhood absence epilepsy (Greek: pykno [absence] + lepsis [seizure])

redshift a shift in the spectral lines of an astronomical body towards longer wavelength values relative to the wavelengths of these lines in the terrestrial spectrum

sagittal time the same as 'time's arrow', a concept defined by Stephen Jay Gould as 'seeing history as an irreversible sequence of unrepeatable events'; opposed to 'time's cycle' in which 'events have no meaning as distinct episodes with causal impact upon a contingent history'

series decay a term used in nuclear science to describe the chain-reaction transformation of a radioactive parent into its daughter product by disintegration, resulting in the gradual decrease in the activity of the parent

stratigraphy the study of the order and relative position of geological strata as a means of historical interpretation

synoecism unification into one state; the Greeks used the term synoecismus to denote the grouping of two or more communities into a single state; it implies the establishment of a political union and centre (whether pre-existing or specially founded), though not necessarily the gathering of population into a single settlement

telematics the set of technologies and services using both information technology and telecommunications for collecting, storing, processing and communicating information

teleoperation the technical term for the remote control of autonomous robots; also known as telemanipulation

teleport (tele + port) an installation that provides access to a range of powerful telecommunications services, such as satellite transmission, teleconferencing, etc.; offices, city areas and regions gain access by private subscription

telepresence an advanced form of teleoperation in which the robot operator gets a sense of being 'on location', even if the robot and the operator are miles apart; control and feedback are done via telemetry sent over wires, optical fibres or radio; in virtual reality the human operator is 'the robot'

teletopical tele + topical, relating to place at a distance, usually by means of telephony

transhumant moving or migrating seasonally

volumetric analysis measurement by volume